Individual Performance Assessment:
An Approach to Criterion-Referenced Test Development

Individual Performance Assessment: An Approach to Criterion-Referenced Test Development

Robert W. Swezey, Ph.D.

Director
Behavioral Sciences Research Center

Reston Publishing Company, Inc.
A Prentice-Hall Company
Reston, Virginia

Library of Congress Cataloging in Publication Data
Swezey, Robert W
   Individual performance assessment: an approach to criterion-
   referenced test development

   Bibliography: p. 159
   Includes index.
   1. Criterion-referenced tests.   I. Title.
LB3060.32.C74S95   371.2'6   80-26777
ISBN 0-8359-3066-1

Editorial/production supervision and interior design
by Barbara J. Gardetto

10 9 8 7 6 5 4 3 2 1

Printed in the United States of America

Contents

Acknowledgments

This book has grown out of a number of interrelated efforts in which I have been involved during the past six years. By far the most important of these was a research project sponsored by the U.S. Army Research Institute for the Behavioral and Social Sciences (ARI) under contract number DACH19-74-C-0018 on which I served as prinicpal investigator. That project resulted in a document known variously as "Guidebook for Developing Criterion-Referenced Tests" (AD A014987), and "Developing Criterion-Referenced Tests" (*JSAS Catalog of Selected Documents in Psychology*, Spring, 1975, Ms. 918) by R. W. Swezey and R. B. Pearlstein. This book draws heavily from that document, as well as from related documents developed during that project (*ARI Technical Report TR-78-A31* by R. B. Pearlstein and R. W. Swezey and *ARI Research Memorandum 75-11* by R. W. Swezey, R. B. Pearlstein, and W. H. Ton).

The second effort was a journal article I wrote when invited by Irv Goldstein to contribute an article on criterion-referenced measurement to a special edition of *Human Factors* (Swezey, 1978), a journal which he edited. The third was a paper presented at the First

International Learning Technology Congress and Exposition on Applied Learning Technology for Human Resources Development, which was subsequently published in the *Journal of Educational Technology Systems* (Swezey, 1977).

These and other efforts have stimulated my interest in criterion-referenced measurement in particular and in individual performance assessement in general. It is my hope that this philosophy of measurement will be more widely applied in performance assessment than is presently the case. I believe that this approach has the potential to solve a great number of individual assessment problems.

Much of the text, as well as many of the tables in this book, were adopted from Swezey and Pearlstein (1975). I am extremely grateful to R. B. Pearlstein whose hard work and insightful thinking contributed greatly to that and, therefore, to this volume. The project monitors of the original ARI documents, Angelo Mirabella and G. Gary Boycan, also provided major support, as did W. H. Ton, a coauthor of one of the 1975 ARI Reports. At that time Pearlstein, Ton, and I were affiliated with Applied Science Associates, where the project was conducted.

Preface

Assessment of individual performance is a topic of major concern in virtually all areas of human endeavor. Requirements to provide accurate, reliable, and valid indices of individual performance are equally as applicable to business and industrial settings as to educational, health, defense, energy, environmental and other facets of society.

The use of a criterion-referenced measurement model to provide the vehicle for performance assessment is an idea whose time has come. As the father of school-age children, I am interested not only in how well my children perform in school relative to their classmates (a norm-referenced issue), but even more importantly, in determining the extent to which they are able to meet externally imposed performance standards (a criterion-referenced issue). It is entirely possible that individuals may perform acceptably relative to other individuals in their group, but that the entire distribution of scores may be skewed such that nobody in the group is able to meet appropriate external performance standards. Such is the case, for example, when it is discovered that high school graduates cannot read acceptably. This issue becomes even more critical in situations where competent performance is mandatory in order to avoid potentially serious consequences that may occur in business, management, industrial, and other settings.

This book presents a method for assessing individual performance via the use of criterion-referenced performance tests. The attempt is to provide a practical, usable methodology, yet one which meets acceptable standards of testing rigor and validity. The technique presented in this book has been tried out in numerous performance assessment situations and is of demonstrated utility.

Robert W. Swezey
at Duck, N.C.
June, 1980

Individual Performance Assessment: An Approach to Criterion-Referenced Test Development

1

Aspects
of
Test Development

The assessment of individual performance is a topic which has been studied for many years. Yet even today, the literatures of psychology and of education contain reference to no more persistent problems than those involving individual performance assessment. In applied situations, no generally accepted model for developing relevant, reliable, and practical individual performance assessment techniques exists. This book discusses a relatively new method for developing such tests termed *criterion-referenced measurement*. This measurement model has shown considerable promise in assessing individual performance in a variety of job-oriented settings.

The individual whose performance is to be evaluated might be a law student, a physician, a radar technician, a sixth grader, or a pianist. The situation in which an individual functions, while important and while most definitely a variable in the equation which describes performance effectiveness, is not the topic of this book. Rather, the area of interest is *individual human performance*, that is, what a person actually *does* (i.e. actions or statements which can be observed, defined, or measured.)

This book is not concerned with attitudes, abilities, or other so-called intervening variables. Instead, the concern is with outcomes of performance which can be objectively identified. While the effects on performance of personality, attitudes, etc., are interesting areas to pursue, they are not of concern here. A variety of sources on such topics are available in the literatures of psychology and of education. See, for example, Fishbein and Azjen, 1975.

THE CRITERION-REFERENCED MEASUREMENT MODEL

Criterion-referenced measurement has been widely considered since the term was originally popularized in 1963 by Robert Glaser. In criterion-referenced measurement, issues which address comparisons among individuals are generally considered irrelevant. Criterion-referenced information is designed to evaluate mastery of a given skill or knowledge, or of given performance objectives. Criterion-referenced measurement has been defined variously in the literature. For purposes of this book, a criterion-referenced test is one in which the score achieved by an individual on a test is interpreted against an external standard. The standard must be a standard other than the distribution of scores of other examinees. Criterion-referenced tests are tests whose items are operational definitions of behavioral or of performance objectives.

Norm-Referenced Measurement

The most widely used model for assessing individual achievement is known as *norm-referenced measurement*. In norm-referenced measurement, the performance of an individual is evaluated relative to the performance of other comparable individuals.

The norm-referenced assessment model has benefited from many years of research and is of demonstrated utility in comparing individuals among themselves and to normative distributions. It is appropriate for a large number of uses, including ranking persons according to their performances on specific tasks, or on other more general topics. In any case, where relative decisions are to be made (promotion, selection, class rankings, pay-level judgments, and other discriminations among individuals), norm-referenced measurement is the preferred model. If, for example, we have a test where local norms have been computed over a period of time, and it is discovered that an individual's test score is at the fortieth percentile of that distribution, we may fairly conclude that the person is doing better than about 40 percent of the individuals in that population. A major emphasis in norm-referenced measurement is to maximize individual differences in order to spread the distribution of test scores. Norm-referenced test items thus are often designed to discriminate among individuals and may be constructed to be of moderate or of extreme difficulty.

Unfortunately, however important and necessary a norm-referenced measurement model may be in performance evaluation, it is not always, by itself, sufficient. Many organizations find themselves in situations where required levels of competence are not being met. It is widely alleged for example, that many high school graduates cannot read acceptably. To the extent that such allegations are correct, they are difficult to detect with a norm-referenced measurement model. The reason is that absolute performance standards are not specified in this model. No external criterion exists against which an individual's performance may be assessed. It is not enough merely to know that Person One is a better performer than Person Two on some task, if the entire distribution of individuals for example, cannot perform appropriately. For such situations, criterion-referenced measurement is appropriate.

Criterion- *vs.* Norm-Referenced Measurement

A criterion-referenced test measures what an individual knows or can do, compared to what he must be able to know or to do, in order to successfully perform a task. An individual's performance thus is compared (or referenced) to an external criterion or performance standard. Such standards are derived directly from an analysis of performances known to be necessary to complete a particular task successfully. In criterion-referenced measurement, an individual's performance is interpreted against an absolute standard, or criterion, without regard to the distribution of scores achieved by other individuals.

To illustrate this distinction between norm-referenced and criterion-referenced measurement, Popham and Husek (1969) have proposed an analogy involving a dog owner who wishes to keep his dog in his back yard. The owner determines the highest fence over which the dog can jump (a criterion-referenced test) and then builds a fence high enough to keep the dog in the back yard. How high the dog can jump relative to other dogs (a norm-referenced test) is irrelevant.

A number of other researchers have made similar distinctions. Glaser and Nitko (1971), for example, have proposed a flexible definition of criterion-referenced measurement:

> A criterion-referenced test is one that is deliberately constructed so as to yield measurements that are directly interpretable in terms of specified performance standards . . . The performance standards are usually specified by defining some domain of tasks that the student should perform. Representative samples of tasks from this domain are organized into a test. Measurements are taken, and are used to make a statement about the performance of each individual relative to that domain.

Livingston (1972) has expanded this definition: "Criterion-referenced . . . (is) used to refer to any test for which a criterion score is specified without reference to the distribution of scores of a group of examinees." Lyons (1972) argued for the use of criterion-referenced measurement as a vital part of training in quality control: "Quality control requires absolute rather than relative criteria. Scores and grades must reflect how many course objectives have been mastered rather than how a student compares with other students."

Panell and Laabs (1979) have also addressed the difference between norm- and criterion-referenced measurement:

> Testing within the standard instructional model usually involves comparing one student's performance with that of others to assign grades. Tests of this kind are known as norm-referenced tests, and recent developments in instructional technology indicate that they are not always appropriate. For example, testing in an individualized instruction program involves the assessment of a student's level of skill or knowledge in more absolute terms for such purposes as diagnosing instructional needs or deciding which sequence of instruction should be followed. A norm-referenced test does not use this type of information. A criterion-referenced test, on the other hand, meets these measurement needs because it references performance to a standard or criterion, rather than to the performance of others. Unfortunately, there are few specific guidelines available for criterion-referenced test construction and the extensive technology available for norm-referenced test construction is not applicable.

OTHER MEASUREMENT MODELS

In addition to norm- and criterion-referenced measurement, a variety of other models for assessing individual performance also exist.

Sherman and Zieky (1974), for example, have listed five additional measurement models:

- Domain-Referenced Measurement
- Objectives-Referenced Measurement
- Decision-Referenced Measurement
- Treatment-Referenced Measurement
- Content-Referenced Measurement

Of these models, three are sufficiently esoteric that we may omit discussion of them here. The interested reader should consult Sherman and Zieky (1974). Domain and objectives-referenced measurement deserve comment.

Domain-Referenced Measurement

Domain-referenced measurement has been defined by Sanders and Murray (1976) as a test in which performance on a task is interpreted by referencing a well-defined set of tasks (i.e. a *domain*). Thus domain-referenced tests emphasize the creation of pools of test items, or of generalized item forms, that are presumed to be representative of a universe of all test items for a well-defined content area (Hively, 1974).

Objectives-Referenced Measurement

Objectives-referenced measurement is defined by Sanders and Murray (1976) as measurement in which performance is interpreted by referencing the specific behavioral objective(s) for which a test item was written. Objectives-referenced tests thus emphasize items which are derived directly from predetermined behaviors. As such, these test items are considered to be operational definitions of the behavioral objectives.

Differences Among the Models

It appears, therefore, that domain- and objectives-referenced measurement refer generally to the *content* that a test was developed to assess. Norm- and criterion-referenced measurement, on the other hand, refer generally to *the way in which a test score is interpreted*, regardless of its content. Criterion-referencing may be viewed as an absolute measurement technique, whereas norm-referencing presumes a relative measurement approach. Domain and objectives orientations suggest item sampling and operational definitions, respectively.

Table 1-1 shows a relationship among these models in which the dimension of content orientation is viewed as being independent from score referent. The cell entries are not necessarily viewed as being mutually exclusive. Thus a given test could, for example, be criterion-referenced while being both objectives- and domain-oriented (in that individual items are appropriately derived from objectives, and the test as a whole adequately samples the content domain). Similarly, a given test score, however it is established, could, if desired, be interpreted in both a normative and in a criterion-referenced fashion. This would happen when both an external performance referent and a distribution of test scores against which a given score may be interpreted exist.

TABLE 1-1

Alternative Measurement Models[1]

| | | Content Orientation | |
		Domain	Objectives
Score	Norm	DN	ON
Referent	Criterion	DC	OC

Note: Cell entries are as follows: DN = Domain-oriented, norm-referenced; DC = domain-oriented, criterion-referenced; ON = objectives-oriented, norm-referenced; and OC = objectives-oriented, criterion-referenced.

[1] Adapted from Swezey (1978).

Most questions involving measurement of individual performance, particularly in job-oriented, or in training-oriented situations, basically involve questions of absolute measurement. They can thus be translated directly into criterion-referenced terms. This book discusses a relatively simple method for constructing criterion-referenced job performance tests (whether domain or objectives oriented). For reviews of the developmental and academic literature in criterion-referenced measurement, consult such sources as: Berk (1980); Swezey (1978); Swezey, Pearlstein and Ton (1975); Sherman and Zieky (1974); Popham (1971); Meskauskas (1976); Hambleton (1974); and Shoemaker (1975). Similarly, other guidance also exists on procedures for developing criterion-referenced tests. See, for example, Panell and Laabs (1979); Guion (1979); Boyd and Shimberg (1971); Sherman and Zieky (1974); and the U.S. Army Training Support Center, Individual Training and Evaluation Directorate (1977).

SOME BASIC ISSUES IN CRITERION-REFERENCED MEASUREMENT

Distinguishing Criterion-Referenced Tests from Norm-Referenced Tests

This book deals with procedures for constructing criterion-referenced performance tests regardless of content. The major issue involved, therefore, is what we have termed *score referent* (i.e. whether test results are interpreted in reference to a specified standard (a criterion-referenced test) or to the distribution of scores of other examinees (a norm-referenced measurement). Those measurements associated with content (see Table 1-1) are not addressed.

As has been mentioned, a criterion-referenced test may be either domain- or objectives-referenced, depending upon the details of the specific testing situation and upon the preference of the individual constructing the test. In criterion-referenced measurement, scores are often recorded in terms of a dichotomous decision (i.e. pass-fail). This decision is determined by the performance of an examinee on a test compared to the performance requirement. If, for example, a performance requirement were established that an examinee must be able to run 100 yards in 12 seconds or less, the performance can be scored dichotomously against this criterion. In such a case, a criterion-referenced test is appropriate. In this example, it is not of interest to determine the extent to which an examinee can run faster or less fast than other examinees. Having administered such a test therefore, one would not necessarily know whether an individual who received a passing score ran faster than another individual who also passed. It would be possible to state categorically, however, that both individuals had sufficient speed to meet the performance requirement.

Criterion-referenced tests may be difficult to distinguish from norm-referenced tests merely by inspecting the test items, since items on both types of tests may appear similar. Both criterion-referenced and norm-referenced tests may use the same types of items, such as multiple-choice items or fill-in-the-blank items. Similarly, both types of tests may use so-called hands-on performance measures such as, "Fix the doorbell so that the bell rings," or, "Connect the battery cable to the battery terminal." Additionally, both types of tests may use simulated performance items such as, "Select the most appropriate dial reading for the air pressure indicator from a series of pictures of air pressure indicators showing various readings." Both criterion- and norm-referenced tests may also include knowledge items such as, "Under what symptoms should a penicillin injection be administered?" or "At what temperature and for how long should lasagna be baked?" Both types of tests may also have skill items such as, "Identify and replace the faulty component on the radio chassis," or "Project the monthly departmental staffing requirements on the form provided." Both norm- and criterion-referenced tests may also use paper and pencil performance items such as "Compute the interest accrued by the savings account," or "Compile a table of contents for the manuscript provided." The point is that merely looking at a test does not provide the necessary data to determine whether or not it is criterion-referenced. In order to determine if a test is criterion-referenced, one must consider such factors as:

- How the test was developed

- The purpose for which the test will be used

- How the test score is interpreted

If a test has the following characteristics, it is most probably criterion-referenced.

- Test scoring must be based upon absolute, rather than upon relative, standards.

- The primary use of the test must be for measuring mastery. That is, the test must be designed to determine whether an individual has mastered specific tasks under examination.

- The test items must be based directly upon known performance objectives associated with the task(s) of interest. If the development of a test can be linked directly to consideration of task(s) that must be actually performed, the test is based upon performance requirements.

Uses of Criterion-Referenced Tests

In criterion-referenced measurement, test items are developed directly from an analysis of tasks to be performed. This is not necessarily the case in norm-referenced testing, where items often address abstract aspects of a task or are knowledge oriented. Criterion-referenced test scores, being typically of a pass-fail nature, do not lend themselves to ordering individuals along a continuum. Thus, if the primary purpose of a test is to select among individuals for, say, a promotion, or for any other normative reason, criterion-referenced measurement is not appropriate. When test information is to be used for purposes of comparing examinees, norm-referenced testing is generally more appropriate than is criterion-referenced measurement. Criterion-referenced measurement, however, is usually the measurement model of choice when judgments are desired about an individual's achievement of specific objectives. In such situations, the major issue of interest involves the extent to which an individual is able to meet externally imposed performance standards rather than the way in which an individual's performance compares to that of others. Thus, if the purpose of a test is to rank individuals or to identify top or bottom performers, a norm-referenced test is probably the technique of choice. If, however, it is necessary to determine what individuals have mastered a given task or objective, a criterion-referenced measurement model is appropriate.

Consider a situation where, for whatever reason, it is necessary to classify only the top 10 percent of a given group of examinees as candidates for additional training. In such a situation, assume that a class is administered a criterion-referenced test having a cut-off score of 90 points (i.e. examinees who score 90 points or above on the test have achieved the minimum acceptable standards). Assume further that 100 points is the maximum possible score (that is, represents a perfect performance). Assume that there are 100 examinees and that they achieve the test scores shown in Table 1-2 on the following page.

In such a situation, a test developer would face a major problem. All examinees in the example have passed the test, and 30 percent have achieved a perfect score. In such a situation how does one identify the top 10 percent? In fact, it is not possible to do so. In such a case, it would be necessary to use some basis other than performance on the test to make the normative decision. Criterion-referenced measurement allows only for decisions involving task mastery. Relative or normative decisions, such as those dealing with selection of outstanding graduates, cannot be made using a criterion-referenced measurement model. Using such a model, one can justifiably comment only upon which examinees have met the prescribed standards, and which have not. Relative or normative decisions must be made on some other basis.

TABLE 1-2

Example Test Data

Number of Examinees Who Achieve This Score	Test Score
30	100
40	99
5	97
5	96
10	95
5	94
3	93
2	91
Total 100	

As Screening Devices

Criterion-referenced tests may be considered appropriate for use as screening devices or as selection instruments in situations where it is anticipated that some portion of the population of individuals tested may be able to perform the required tasks without prior training. If a person can perform a task at the required proficiency level as demonstrated by a valid criterion-referenced test, that person has demonstrated mastery on the task(s) under examination even though he may not have completed prerequisite training (that may be required for others). That is, criterion-referenced tests may be used to distinguish those individuals whose input repertoire of skills or knowledge already meets the requirements for task mastery from those whose input repertoire does not. Similarly, criterion-referenced tests may be used to determine the appropriate point in a training cycle for an individual to begin training. Once the input repertoire of an examinee is known, as measured by a valid criterion-referenced test, it may be possible for that person to skip aspects of training on which he has previously demonstrated mastery. If an individual must possess certain entry behaviors prior to beginning an advanced course, it may be appropriate to examine that individual using a criterion-referenced test prior to his beginning the instruction. A beginner's test, for instance, is often used as a screening device in advanced swimming instruction. If an individual can pass such a screening test, it is presumed that the individual has the necessary knowledge and/or the basic skills required to begin the advanced swimming course.

Criterion-referenced tests may also be used as screening devices to determine the extent to which an individual's performance may already meet the standards required for successful performance of a given task. If for instance, an individual has already mastered many of the required behaviors in a given training curriculum, it may be appropriate to train the individual on only those tasks where mastery requirements have not been met. If an individual is able to achieve a mastery level score on a test that is required for graduation from a training curriculum, valuable time and resources may be saved by not training that individual on previously mastered tasks.

As Aids in Diagnosis

Criterion-referenced tests may be used as diagnostic aids for determining placement of individuals in advanced instruction, or for determining appropriate areas of remediation. A criterion-referenced test whose content is based upon objectives required for successful task performance may be used to diagnose deficiences of individuals who fail to meet specified performance standards. It is therefore possible to construct criterion-referenced tests for diagnostic purposes, in order to determine areas in which an individual's performance is weak (i.e. does not meet mastery standards), or for use in later remediation, placement, or curriculum-branching decisions. A diagnostic criterion-referenced test in the area of income tax preparation, for example, may demonstrate deficiencies in ability to perform the procedures required for computing the medical deduction on IRS Form 1040. In such a case, remediation would focus on medical deductions, since additional instruction would not be required for those other aspects of tax preparation where the individual has demonstrated mastery.

In Evaluating Instruction

Another purpose for which criterion-referenced tests may be constructed is for use in evaluating instructional programs in terms of their adequacy for preparing trainees to perform required tasks. In such a situation, criterion-referenced test results collected from a group of examinees may be assessed in terms of the extent to which the number of individuals graduating from an instructional program (i.e. demonstrating mastery), is considered satisfactory. If fewer individuals than are considered appropriate graduate (i.e. master the content necessary for graduation), then an argument may be made that the instructional program may be deficient in some way. Further, areas where improvement is indicated may be observed from examining the aspects of a task or tasks that the sample of individuals has not mastered. A simplified design to aid in determining adequacy of an instructional program using criterion-referenced tests, for example, may include such steps as:

- Identify an appropriate sample of individuals who cannot adequately perform required tasks (i.e. are not masters).

- Train these individuals.

- Retest the sample after training, using the same criterion-referenced test employed prior to training.

If an instructional program is adequate, most people should be able to achieve mastery after completion of training.

The norm-referenced measurement model is less appropriate for evaluating instructional programs, since the wide test score variances that may occur both before and after training are not necessarily relevant to the question of interest. Since criterion-referenced tests designed for such a purpose are presumably based directly upon instructional objectives, and since the basic question of interest is whether or not a training program has successfully presented information compatible with performing the instructional objectives, the criterion-referenced measurement model provides data that do have direct relevance to this question.

COST EFFECTIVENESS ISSUES

Cost effectiveness of criterion-referenced tests is often a major issue. Criterion-referenced tests may, in general, be considerably more costly to develop than are comparable norm-referenced tests. The reason is due largely to the requirement that test items and objectives be carefully derived, specified, and operationally defined. Additionally, increased administration costs may result from the use of expensive equipment, facilities, and simulators, particularly in situations where hands-on tests are required. Nevertheless, it may well be the case that criterion-referenced measurement is more cost effective than other testing alternatives in the long run, particularly where there is genuine need to assess ability to perform specific tasks.

Indirect approaches to criterion-referenced measurement via such techniques as symbolic testing (Osborn, 1970, for example) may aid in alleviating the high costs associated with criterion-referenced test development. Such approaches involve the development of two tests (at different levels of measurement fidelity) for each objective, and subsequent validation of the indirect (symbolic) measures against the performance measures. Justification for such approaches centers on savings in administrative time and costs. Nevertheless, direct development of criterion-referenced tests appears appropriate if a requirement exists to insure that individuals will be able to perform adequately on the tasks under examination. When a need exists to establish absolute measures of performance, criterion-referenced measurement appears to be the technique of choice.

AN OVERVIEW OF THE TEST CONSTRUCTION PROCESS PRESENTED IN THIS BOOK

There is no single correct way to construct a criterion-referenced performance test. The construction process outlined in this book, however, will, if followed, enable the construction of reliable and valid criterion-referenced tests. It is a relatively simple, straightforward method of test construction, yet one which meets rigorous validity and reliability standards. Other methods of constructing criterion-referenced tests are also available. One that is very similar in concept to the approach taken in this book has been presented by Panell and Laabs (1979). Others have been described by Sherman and Zieky (1974), and by Boyd and Shimberg (1971), among others.

The criterion-referenced test construction process presented in this book is designed to be applicable in diverse types of testing situations and to widely varying subject matter. The procedures presented are designed to be simple and efficient and to lead to valid, reliable criterion-referenced tests that will accurately measure individual performance. An outline of the major steps involved in construction and application of criterion-referenced job performance tests is presented below. Each step is described in detail in the following chapters.

Step 1: Evaluate Inputs to the Criterion-Referenced Test Development Process. Adequate task analyses are necessary inputs to the development of accurate and reliable criterion-referenced tests. Additionally, a criterion-referenced test developer must have available operationally stated performance objectives based upon the task analyses. The first step of the test development process described in this book requires that the adequacy of these objectives be evaluated. Objectives found to be inadequate are then revised or discarded. In assessing the adequacy of objectives, a criterion-referenced test developer independently evaluates three separate components of an adequate objective: performances, conditions, and standards. *Performances* refer to what an objective requires the examinee to know and/or to do. *Conditions* refer to the situations under which an examinee's performance is evaluated. *Standards* refers to the level of performance required in order to demonstrate satisfactory achievement of an objective.

Step 2: Planning the Test.   Before actually writing test items, it is necessary to establish an overall plan for the test. Three factors are considered in establishing a plan for constructing criterion-referenced tests.

- The ways in which practical constraints such as time, personnel availability, and cost may affect test construction.

- Item format and fidelity issues (i.e. the realism of the test and its items). Examples of various types of item formats include written items, hands-on performance items, simulated performance items, measures of how a performance is accomplished, process items, and product items.

- Number of items. This issue involves considerations concerning how many items a test should include, as well as the appropriate number of items required to assess each objective within a test.

Step 3: Developing a Pool of Items.   The procedures described in this book recommend that at least two items be created for each item requirement in the test plan. In this way, a pool of items is created from which the best items (i.e. those that are empirically determined to best discriminate between masters and non-masters of the subject matter content) may be selected. Each item in the pool must be considered from the perspective of such issues as:

- Is the item clear and unambiguous?

- Does the item adequately reflect the objective from which it was created?

- Is the item at an appropriate level of fidelity (realism) as specified by the test plan?

- Is the item reasonably easy to administer and score?

During the item development phase of test construction, one also prepares a plan for administering the items as well as a general administration procedure for the test.

Step 4: Selection of Final Criterion-Referenced Test Items. The item pool must be tried out, and reviewed by content experts. Poor or redundant items are revised or discarded as appropriate. It may also be necessary to create additional items if the tryout and content review eliminate items which cause gaps in the test plan (i.e. where objectives remain that are not adequately covered by items).

Step 5: Test Administration and Scoring. The next step in the process of developing a criterion-referenced test involves the creation of scoring standards and administrative procedures for each item and for the overall test. Administration and scoring procedures should be sufficiently clear and unambiguous that others can administer the test reliably and with minimal measurement error. It is also necessary to determine scoring procedures and cut-off levels necessary to establish acceptable scores for each objective and for the test at large.

Step 6: Reliability Measurement. Reliability of a criterion-referenced test is determined by establishing its stability over repeated administrations (retests). Test-retest reliability, as recommended in this book, involves determination of the extent to which test scores remain similar over repeated administrations.

Step 7: Validity Measurement. Validity is the extent to which a test accurately measures the objective(s) it was designed to assess. When a test is repeatedly administered to a sample of examinees, it may measure their behaviors consistently (i.e. reliably) but may be assessing issues other than those for which it was designed. In such a situation, the test could be considered reliable, but not valid. This book describes empirical procedures for assessing the validity of a test. If a test (or various included items) is shown to have low validity, it must be revised, discarded, or improved in order to achieve acceptable validity standards.

This book presents a straightforward, feasible approach for developing and validating criterion-referenced tests. It also provides references to relevant literature for further consideration by interested readers. Many sophisticated models exist for the development and validation of individual performance assessment indices. The problem with many of these models is that their esoteric nature and/or complicated procedures often serve to minimize their utility. Classroom teachers and industrial trainers, for example, rarely consider questions of test reliability and validity in their development activities. One reason for this may be that the establishment of test reliability and validity often involves both complicated procedures and a great deal of work. It is often neither cost effective nor time effective for such test developers to compute item statistics and/or test reliability and validity coefficients. A typical approach to test development in applied performance testing situations is simply:

1. To determine the domains that one wants to test.

2. To write a number of test items relevant to that domain.

3. To administer the test to the appropriate population.

4. To score the test as objectively and as unbiased as possible.

5. To arbitrarily establish cutting points for the grade distribution.

This may be a reasonable approach if one's purpose in developing a test is a norm- or domain-referenced one. If, however, one is concerned about objectives- and criterion-referenced measurement, the approach is generally inadequate. This book addresses the topic of development and construction of reliable, valid criterion-referenced performance tests.

SUMMARY

In this chapter, the concept of criterion-referenced measurement has been introduced, and differentiated from other measurement models such as norm-, domain-, and objectives-referenced measurement. A rationale for the use of criterion-referenced measurement has been presented, and methods for distinguishing criterion-referenced tests from norm-referenced tests have been described. Various uses of criterion-referenced tests have been discussed, including such applications as screening devices, aids in diagnosis, and evaluating instruction.

The issue of cost-effective testing has been raised, and its impacts in criterion-referenced measurement, introduced. Finally, an overview of the test construction process presented in this book has been outlined as follows:

- Step 1: Evaluate inputs to the criterion-referenced test development process
- Step 2: Planning the test
- Step 3: Developing a pool of items
- Step 4: Selection of final criterion-referenced test items
- Step 5: Test administration and scoring
- Step 6: Reliability measurement
- Step 7: Validity measurement

These steps parallel the chapter discussions in the remainder of the book, with the single exception being that steps 6 and 7 are combined in the final chapter.

2

Evaluating Inputs to the Criterion-Referenced Test Development Process

The criterion-referenced measurement model is a relatively recent addition to the area of individual performance assessment. Thus, construction methodology issues vary widely, and numerous points of view exist on virtually all aspects of criterion-referenced construction methodology. See, for example, Swezey, Pearlstein, and Ton (1975). In criterion-referenced measurement, methodological issues are not nearly so well defined nor researched as is the case with the norm-referenced model, which has benefited from decades of research and application. Nevertheless, general guidelines can be established for the construction of criterion-referenced job performance tests.

TASK ANALYSIS

In order to develop a valid criterion-referenced test which is based upon adequate performance objectives, a thorough task analysis is a necessary prerequisite. Such an analysis enables identification of the critical elements required for successful task performance and provides for analysis of the appropriate tasks into their component skills and knowledges.

Numerous task analytic procedures exist. See for instance, Fine and Wiley (1971); Miller (1966); and Chenzoff and Folley (1965). Such analyses are necessary preliminary activities in criterion-referenced test development. The actual conduct of task analyses may be outside a test developer's particular domain of activity, and therefore, also outside of the domain of this book; in order to develop an adequate criterion-referenced test, a developer must have access to task information on:

- Required skills and knowledges

- Necessary performances that must be accomplished

- Criteria associated with each performance that is identified.

- Conditions under which each performance must be accomplished

Lacking such data, a developer cannot adequately define performance objectives for test development, and consequently cannot perform the subsequent steps in the processes involved in criterion-referenced test construction. In order to construct usable, accurate, and valid criterion-referenced tests, adequate task analyses are necessary input data.

OBJECTIVE DEVELOPMENT

Another preliminary step in the criterion-referenced test development process involves establishment of performance objectives for each appropriate task. Data derived from task analyses are used in the process of objective development. This book deals only briefly with the topic of objective development. Interested readers are referred to a series of books by Mager (1962, 1973) and Mager and Pipe, (1970) for additional information. The test development process discussed in this book assumes that a test developer already has available appropriate performance objectives for use in developing a test. Thus, the two preliminary steps in criterion-referenced test preparation (task analysis and preparation of objectives) are not treated directly here.

Assuming that adequate objectives have been obtained for use in developing tests, an initial test development activity involves matching test items to the objectives. An implicit assumption, of course, is that the objectives themselves adequately represent actual job tasks. If this assumption is violated, the resulting criterion-referenced test will lack validity. If, however, the assumption is accurate and the test developer competently matches items to these objectives, a particular type of test validity (termed *content validity*—discussed in Chapter 7) will necessarily be achieved. A test developer must therefore be knowledgeable about both quality standards for objectives and about task analysis techniques in order to adequately assess objectives in terms of their suitability for the construction of criterion-referenced tests.

Objectives are detailed descriptions of the specific behaviors that a test is designed to assess. Objectives indicate the performance(s) an individual must accomplish in order to successfully perform required tasks or to complete a required program. This chapter discusses the components of adequately prepared objectives and describes an approach for evaluating the adequacy of objectives as inputs to the development of criterion-referenced tests.

Adequate objectives typically have several distinguishing features: they are involved with only one concept per objective; are specific in terms of their primary intent; include indicators of the necessary performance(s) which are direct and readily achievable; and are specified in precise, operational terms. If objectives are inadequate, the test items developed from the objectives will also be inadequate and, as a result, the validity of the entire criterion-referenced test will be diminished.

COMPONENTS OF AN ADEQUATE OBJECTIVE

Before developing a test, it is appropriate to consider closely the objectives to be used as the basis of the test items. A good objective can be partitioned into three integral components, termed *performances*, *conditions*, and *standards*. These components may also be known by various other names. Table 2-1 shows some synonyms for the three components of an adequate objective.

TABLE 2-1

Synonyms for Components of an Objective

Performance	Condition	Standard
• Activity	• Test Condition	• Criterion
• Action	• Required Equipment	• Cut-off
• Skill	• Required Facilities	• Passing grade
• Knowledge	• Required Personnel	• Requirement
• Response	• Required Materials	• Go, no-go standards
• Task	• Environment	
• Reaction	• Set-up	
	• Job Condition	

Clearly Stated Performance Objectives

Every adequate objective must unambiguously state precisely what performances an individual must accomplish in order to adequately achieve the intent of the objective. The statement of performance must be sufficiently clear for that performance to actually be tested. Examples of adequately stated performances might include:

- *Add* the number 48,713 to the number 89,562

- *Compute* the distance from point A to point B on the map provided

- *Focus* the camera

- *Install* the carburetor

- *Lock* the safe

- *Identify* the faulty component

- *Write* a proposal

- *Construct* a picture frame

As is evident in these examples, every adequate statement of performance includes an action verb. The verb is generally the key to the performance required by the objective. It indicates what must actually be accomplished in order to complete the requirements included in the objective. For example, in the statement, "Set the thermostat so that the temperature level reads 70 degrees," the action verb is "set." It is possible to actually test an individual's ability to set a thermostat. If, on the other hand, the statement of performance had read, "Understand the advantages of a 70-degree household temperature," it would be difficult to determine how to test the objective. At best, it is extremely difficult to test an examinee's understanding of advantages. It is, therefore, important that an action verb be specified as an indicator of performance. Setting a thermostat can be measured accurately, whereas "understanding advantages" cannot.

At this point it is necessary, however, to insert a caveat. It is entirely possible that an action verb may not, by itself, directly specify the performance to be accomplished. It may, for example, merely suggest a performance. In such situations, the verb serves as an *indicator* of the performances in question. Anytime that it is not possible to directly observe the required performance, an indicator of that performance must be provided.

Consider the following example. Assume a statement of performance required that a person multiply two three-digit numbers. In this case, the term *multiply* is an action verb. It is clear that the performance required by the objective is multiplication. At issue, however, is the way in which one demonstrates that the multiplication has in fact been achieved, since it is not possible to actually observe the act of multiplication. In such a case obviously an indicator must be supplied. A better objective might state, "Multiply the two three-digit numbers, and *record the answer in the space provided.*" In this case, recording is the observable action; however, the primary intent of the objective is multiplying, not recording. If a statement of performance calls for an action (i.e. has a defined main intent) but that action is not directly observable, then an indicator of the action must be added to the objective. In this example, writing the answer in the provided space indicates whether or not the multiplication has been successfully accomplished.

Accurate Condition Specifications

Every objective should also include a statement of the conditions under which the performance is to be demonstrated. Statements of conditions should indicate:

- What facilities or equipment are available for the examinee to use in performing the item

- Circumstances under which the performance is to be demonstrated

- Limitations or special instructions affecting the performance.

It is important for each objective to accurately specify all conditions which may affect performance. Without statements which specify conditions, it is difficult to understand precisely what performances are to be tested. Suppose, for example, that an objective stated, "Compute the square root of the number 421." Assume that the examinee has previously received training in the computation of square roots, but has always had access to a square root table from which to interpolate. If no square root table (or calculator) is provided in the test, and conditions were not previously specified, the examinee would not know what to expect, and the test developer may not know precisely what to test. Precise specification of the conditions under which a performance must be demonstrated is critical for a good objective.

Situations may also arise where a performance must be demonstrated under multiple conditions. In such cases, this requirement must be specified in the objective. If, for example, an examinee must be able to pilot an aircraft under both visual and instrument conditions, such a requirement must be stated in the objective. In many situations, a performance must be demonstrated under *any* condition. Such situations often occur in the case of critical objectives. Consider for example, the requirements imposed upon fire-fighting units. The individuals involved must be able to perform their tasks under any conditions, regardless of the context or situation in which a fire occurs. Whatever the case, objectives must clearly specify conditions under which specified performances must be accomplished. If conditions are restricted, the objective must so state. If a performance must be accomplished under any condition, the objective must also clearly state this requirement.

Following are several statements which provide adequate definitions of conditions:

- "Given the diameter of a circle and the appropriate formula, compute the circumference."

- "Compare the color of paint of the samples on the assembly line to the standard color provided for reference."

- "Measure the 2x4 to a length of 7 feet using the tape measure provided."

- "Maintain the temperature of the fire at 1400 degrees

Fahrenheit, according to the installed thermometer."

- Replace the sweep second hand on the watch face without causing damage to the hour and minute hands."

- "Prepare a 20-minute speech for the division director which covers all points included in the materials provided."

Precisely Stated Standards

As is the case with performances and conditions, an adequately stated objective must also unambiguously indicate the standard against which the performance will be evaluated. Standards may be described in terms of such measures as: time, errors, level of quality, and rate. If, for example, an objective required that an office worker be able to operate a copying machine under standard office conditions, it is virtually impossible to know precisely what to test or how to score performance. In such a case, would it be appropriate to test for use of the sorting device on the office copier, or use of the two-sided copying capability, or use of the color-copying capability, or use of the feeding mechanism? Obviously, the objective is lacking clear statements both of performance and of standards. A more complete objective might state, "Copy the two-sided colored document provided, and collate the reproduced pages into three complete copies, using all appropriate machine features, with all pages arranged properly, in 6 minutes." In this objective, both the performances and the standard (all pages properly arranged within 6 minutes) are precisely stated.

Various types of standards can be developed to indicate ways in which a performance must be accomplished or a product completed. Table 2-2 shows several types of standards. An objective should specify at least one of the types of standards shown in Table 2-2. In many situations an adequate objective may combine several of the types of standards shown.

Another source of discussion of the topic areas covered in this chapter that uses slightly different terms than those employed here is provided by Mager (1962). Mager's book discusses such topic areas as: definition of objectives, the importance of being explicit about objectives, the necessary quality of meaningful communication in adequate objectives, and identification of terminal behaviors. Mager's little volume is highly recommended for those who wish additional information on the establishment of objectives, their performances, conditions, and standards.

TABLE 2-2

Various Types of Standards

Category	Type	Example
Quantity	Production	Correct 25 essay examination papers
Quality	Tolerance level	Boresight all three aiming reticles to a ±1 degree tolerance level
Rate	Quantity per unit of time	Code five optical scanning forms per hour
Time	Performance occurs at a specified speed	Construct the frame in 45 minutes
Errors	Record mistakes or incomplete performances	Complete all steps in the maintenance checklist
Quality	Subjective quality	Rate the figure skating exhibition on a six-point scale
Errors	Zero error	Balance the checking account

SEPARATING AN OBJECTIVE INTO ITS COMPONENT PARTS

Separating an objective into its components is a necessary initial step in constructing adequate test items. As an example of this process, consider a situation where an examinee is provided with a plat of a building lot and a ruler, and is asked to use these items to determine the distance in feet from the right-front corner of the house to the right-front corner of the lot, and to state the correct answer within plus or minus one foot in three minutes or less. Following is how such an objective might be divided into its three components:

- **Performances**: Essentially two performances are called for in the objective. Measuring the distance in inches using the ruler, and converting the inches to feet using the scale of measurement information printed on the plat. If the lot length is 150 feet, and measures 15 inches on the plat, it is possible to convert inches to feet on a one-inch-to-one-foot basis. Performances therefore require: establishment of the scale of measurement of the plat, measurement of the distance from the right-front corner of the house to the right-front corner of the lot in inches, and conversion of the measurement back to feet, reporting within a plus or minus one foot tolerance level. In this case, measuring inches and converting inches to feet are the required performances, while the indicator of the performance is the statement specifying the number of feet. In such a situation, the best way to determine whether the examinee has correctly accomplished the performance is via the indicator (i.e. stating the correct answer within plus or minus one foot).

- **Conditions**: The conditions given in this objective include the plat with its scale of measurement, and the ruler. In this example, environmental conditions are minimal and therefore are not specified.

- **Standards**: Two standards are stated in the objective. The examinee must state the correct number of feet within a tolerance limit of plus or minus one foot, and must perform the task within three minutes.

Now consider another objective: "Using the wrecker and sling provided, the examinee must operate the wrecker hoist and secure an automobile in place for towing, following the appropriate procedures for that specific make, body style, and year of automobile, as specified in the hoist operator's manual.

Dividing this objective into its parts, we obtain:

- **Performance**: The required performance is operation of the hoist. In this case the performance may be directly observed and, therefore, requires no indicator.

- **Conditions**: A number of conditions are stated in this objective:

  1. The equipment to be used is specified.

  2. The equipment to be operated upon (the automobile) is also specified.

  3. Special instructions are provided; that is, the instruction in the hoist operator's manual for the specific year, make, and body style of the automobile.

- **Standard**: A hoisted automobile that is securely attached to the wrecker. In this objective, no performance time is stated because time limits are not considered critical to accomplishment of the objective.

As is evident from these examples, objectives may vary widely in the extent to which they provide operational descriptions of the required performances, conditions, and standards. It may, for various objectives, be more or less difficult to extract the relevant information in a fashion that facilitates operational definitions of performances, conditions, and standards. Separating objectives into their components is a critical step in the establishment of adequate criterion-referenced test items.

OTHER ASPECTS OF OBJECTIVES

The mere fact that an objective has adequately defined performances, conditions, and standards, however, does not necessarily imply that the objective is totally suitable. Other considerations may also be appropriate for assessing objective adequacy. Additional items for consideration include:

- Each objective should cover a single task only (and not a combination of tasks).

- Performance indicators should be simple, direct and part of the trainee's repertoire of behavior.

- The main intent of the objective must be clear.

- Performances, conditions, and standards specified in the objective must be described in precise, operational terms.

Unitary Objectives

Compound objectives also must be broken down into unitary objectives, and even further, into their components, before proceeding with test item development. It is essentially impossible to develop reliable and valid test items which directly match objectives unless the objectives themselves are unitary. In order to determine whether or not an objective is unitary, one looks at the performance aspect of the objective that is described by the action verb. If the action verb does not specify a unitary performance, it will be necessary to break the objective down further into performance components each of which specifies a unitary performance. This can be accomplished by considering two questions:

- Are the tasks independent? That is, successful performance on one task should not require successful performance on a preceding task(s).

- Does each objective call for a performance on only one task?

If the answer to either or both of the above questions is no, the objective is not unitary, and it should be specified more precisely. Below are listed the performance portions of some objectives that appear to be unitary:

- "Perform the appropriate turn-on procedures for the computer terminal as specified in the operations manual."

- "Perform the necessary check-out activities to assure that the computer terminal is operating properly, as specified in the operations manual."

- "Perform maintenance activities on the computer terminal as specified in the maintenance manual."

In this case the objectives appear to be unitary. The performances required in the three examples involve turn-on procedures, check-out procedures, and maintenance, respectively.

Each of these operations is relatively independent of the others, and therefore, need not be broken down into more unitary performances.

Consider, however, the following objectives which read, in part:

- "Treat for shock."

- "Treat for fracture of the radius."

- "Clean the wound."

- "Administer mouth-to-mouth resuscitation."

- "Control arterial bleeding."

- "Perform first aid for face wounds, neck wounds, and upper body wounds."

Note in the above examples that the last objective calls for performance on a number of tasks, while the preceding objectives are unitary. Additionally, there appears to be considerable overlap among the listed objectives. Controlling arterial bleeding, for instance, is one of the components of treating face, neck, and upper body wounds. Treatment for shock is a general requirement for virtually all first aid practices. It is important to review objectives thoroughly to check for such faults as overlap and lack of unitary performances.

Clarity of Intent

A second major consideration in assessing adequacy of objectives is to determine that the intent of the objective is unambiguous. This may be accomplished by considering the performance statement for each objective and ensuring that the performance statement calls specifically for the performance intended by the objective. If this appears to be the case, in all probability the intent of the objective is clear. If not however, the performance called for may be missing the main point or intent of the objective, or is not of an observable nature. It is important to ensure that the intent of each objective is itself clear and operationally stated. Below are two examples of performance statements in which the intent is clearly and unambiguously specified, and is a directly observable performance.

- **"Unlock the bank vault."** In this case unlocking is a directly observable performance, and the main intent of the objective is that the vault be unlocked.

- **"Climb the telephone pole."** Again, the performance called for is climbing a pole and that is the main intent. It is possible to directly observe the behavior of pole climbing.

Following is an example of performance statement in which the main intent of the objective is clearly stated; however, the required performance is an indicator:

- **"Circle the picture of the appropriate handsaw for use in cutting across the grain of a piece of wood."**

In this case, the intent of the objective is to demonstrate recognition of a cross-cut saw, and to discriminate it from a rip saw. Circling the picture is not the primary intent of the objective, but is merely the performance indicator employed. If the objective were written in a different format, it might require that the examinee actually select a cross-cut saw from among several available types of saws. In this case, the intent would be selection of a cross-cut saw, and would be directly observable. There would be no performance indicator.

Consider an example of a performance statement in which the intent of the objective is unclear, and for which no performance indicator is provided:

- "Be aware of techniques for constructing behavioral objectives." The problem with this performance statement is that being aware of something is ambiguous. How does one measure awareness? Is the examinee actually supposed to construct behavioral objectives? What are the inputs? Is a task analysis available, or is the intent merely to be able to identify behavioral objectives that have been correctly constructed? Obviously, it is impossible to tell. "Being aware" is sufficiently ambiguous that it cannot be measured operationally. In this example also, no indicator is provided to demonstrate measurement of the act of being aware.

Consider another example:

- "Demonstrate an understanding of the differences between operant and respondent conditioning."

As in the previous example, the intent of the objective is unclear. "Demonstrating an understanding" is sufficiently ambiguous that one must devise an indicator in order to operationalize the performance.

It is also important to demonstrate the main intent of an objective, even when an indicator is provided. This is necessary because the test developer's job in constructing items includes consideration of the extent to which an indicator actually indicates the performances required by the intent of the objective. To the extent it does not, the indicator must be revised.

Here is an example of a performance objective with a clear indicator, but with an ambiguous intent:

- "Place a check mark beside the tools appropriate for carburetor maintenance."

In this example the indicator (i.e. placing a check mark) is clear; however, the intent of the objective is ambiguous. It is unknown as to what precisely is meant by carburetor maintenance. Does the term *maintenance* refer to trouble-shooting the carburetor? Removal of the carburetor? Removal and repair of the carburetor? All of the above? It is not possible to tell on the basis of the objective alone since its intent is unclear. The test developer, therefore, does not know precisely what the indicator is supposed to indicate.

Consider another example:

- "Demonstrate an understanding of good speech writing skills by listing the three main topics in the speech provided."

Again, the intent of the objective is ambiguous, but the performance indicator is clear. Listing is a directly observable act that can be measured. However, listing the three main topics in a speech does not necessarily demonstrate an *understanding* of speech writing skills. It is unclear as to what is meant by "demonstrate an understanding," and the extent to which speech writing is involved. The indicator provides no help in determining the intent of the objective. In a situation such as this, the intent of the objective should be clarified, and an indicator selected that is appropriate to the main intent.

A better objective might be:

- "Name the three topics in Lincoln's Gettysburg address."

In this situation (assuming that the three main topics were previously agreed upon by a board of judges) the objective requires that the examinee name those topics. Here, the indicator (i.e naming) and the intent (i.e. recognizing the three main topics in a speech) are compatible. The point of this discussion is that adequate performance objectives must have clear main intents and that indicators must be compatible with the intents. The importance of this requirement cannot be overemphasized in developing performance objectives.

Performance Indicator Simplicity

For objectives where the intent is clear and the required performance is readily observable, indicators are unnecessary. Mager (1973) terms such objectives *overt*. That is, the required performances are overt (directly observable) as a function of the way the objective is stated, and of the clarity of the main intent. Situations where the objectives are not directly observable and where performance indicators are therefore necessary are termed *covert* by Mager. That is, the intent of the objective is covert, and in order to make it operational (overt) an indicator is required. Covert main intents require indicators because their required performances are not directly observable. The covert intent of an objective indicates an unobservable event with which the objective is concerned, while the indicator suggests how to measure the intent.

If an objective's intent is measured via an indicator, it is necessary to establish that the indicator is itself, appropriate. A good indicator has three characteristics:

- It is simple. It is uncomplicated and unambiguous. The intent is not obscured by unnecessary complexity.

- It is direct. The indicator is straightforward. It allows determination of the extent to which the objective's intent has been satisfied, without resorting to inferences.

- It is within the normal repertoire of behavior of the examinee. The examinee should normally be able to perform the behavior required by the indicator. The indicator itself should not require training or skill beyond that which the examinee possesses at the time of testing. If an indicator is not a part of an examinee's repertoire of behavior, and the examinee fails an item that includes the indicator, it is impossible to determine whether the failure was because the examinee could not perform the indicator or because he was unable to perform the main intent of the item.

As an example:

- "Show that you can recognize the major organs of the human body by drawing a picture of each organ beside the names of the organs provided on the handout."

In this situation, the intent of the objective involves recognition of body organs. The indicator of recognition requires drawing pictures of the organs. The implicit assumption is that an individual who can draw a picture of an organ and who can identify its correct name, can in fact, recognize the organ. Although this assumption is probably correct, the indicator (i.e. drawing a picture) may not be within the repertoire of behavior of the examinee. It is possible that an examinee could recognize body organs, but be a poor artist. The indicator is inappropriate for the intent of the objective since an examinee could fail to satisfy the objective simply due to inadequate drawing ability. The indicator is a poor one for a second reason, also. The intent emphasizes *recognition* behavior, although the indicator requires that the examinee *recall* from memory the shape of each organ and then draw the organ. Recognition is a less stringent standard than recall. It is possible, therefore, that examinees who may in fact be able to *recognize* organs of the body may not be able to *recall* them, to say nothing about their ability to draw the organs. In this situation, a better performance indicator, appropriate for the main intent, would involve naming body organs from presented pictures.

Consider another example:

- "Be able to recognize correctly filled out application forms by filling out examples of them yourself."

Again, the main intent of the objective is recognition of correctly filled out forms. Asking the examinee to actually fill out the forms is neither a simple nor a direct measure of recognition behavior. Here, the required performance is relatively complex (i.e. filling out the forms), whereas the intent of the objective is relatively simple (i.e. recognizing forms which are correctly filled out). In this case, the indicator is less likely to be a part of the individual's repertoire of behavior than is the main intent. This is precisely the opposite of the way things should be.

A better objective would be:

- "Sort through the pile of completed applications and separate those that are correctly completed from those that are not."

In this case, all that is required of the examinee is to sort through the documents and to separate those that are correctly completed from those that are not. This is a simple and direct indicator of behavior that is compatible with the intent of the objective. It is also within the normal behavioral repertoire of most examinees. The point is that if the main intent of an objective is not directly observable (i.e. the objective is covert, for whatever reason) it is important to ensure that an appropriate indicator of the intent is included in the objective. Such an indicator should be simple and direct and part of the examinee's repertoire of behavior. If the indicators presented in an objective are inadequate, it is necessary to modify them in order to create new indicators which are adequate.

Precision in Performances, Conditions, and Standards

Another aspect of adequate objectives involves the necessity to ensure that the behaviors required by objectives are specified in precise operational terms. Essentially, this requires that each statement be readily translatable into actions. Table 2-3, for example, shows a list of inadequate verbs (i.e. verbs that do not operationally specify an action) paired with comparable action verbs that might correctly be employed to assess the main intent of an objective. It is important to point out that many additional verbs may also be appropriate for use in criterion-referenced test development, but are not included in Table 2-3 for reasons of brevity.

TABLE 2-3

Example Verbs

Inadequate Verbs	Action Verbs
Understand	Write
Appreciate	Check off
Consider	State
Determine	Label
Realize	Set
Recognize	Point to

In some situations, what may appear to be an appropriate action verb may not be suitable. It is, therefore, important to identify an appropriate action verb that is compatible with the intent of an objective, and that specifies precisely the required actions.

In addition to performance statements, statements of conditions and of standards must also be specified in precise operational terms. If a given objective requires that a performance be conducted in the rain, or in conditions having wind velocities below 20 miles an hour, such situations should be specifically stated. Similarly, if standards require measurement within plus or minus two degrees of arc, or to the nearest minute, such standards should also be specified. Table 2-4 provides examples of statements of conditions and of standards, some that are specified in precise operational terms, and others that are not. An adequate standard will indicate, as precisely as possible, the acceptable performance criteria for scoring a criterion-referenced test item. Mere approximation is insufficient. When writing an item, the test developer must determine how to best comply with the standard prescribed in the objective. For example, if the standard prescribes a 90 percent accuracy criterion, the test developer must determine whether this means nine out of ten, 90 out of 100, 36 out of 40, etc., based upon an assessment of the requirements of the situation and of the available resources.

TABLE 2-4

Example Conditions and Standards

	Inadequate	*Adequate*
Conditions	"Using appropriate equipment"	"Using the 7/16-inch socket and socket wrench provided"
	"In a remote location"	"At the Western Ridge firing range"
	"In extreme temperatures"	"Below −10° Celcius"
	"At normal altitudes"	"Between sea level and 30,000 feet"
Standards	"Under normal time conditions"	"Within five minutes"
	"Record the answer"	"Calculate to six decimal places and round back to five"
	"Accurate typing"	"Typing at 75 words per minute with no errors"
	"Acceptable quality"	"Achieve a rating of eight on ten point scale"

It is important to determine whether the conditions and standards specified in an objective actually specify all information required to write an accurate test item. If not, it will be necessary to supply appropriate conditions and/or standards. If conditions and standards in a final test item are ambiguous and imprecise, it is very likely that an inadequate test will result. Precise definitions are imperative in criterion-referenced measurement.

SUMMARY

This chapter has discussed how objectives may be divided into their three main component parts (performances, conditions and standards), and has provided several examples of this process. Methods for evaluating the adequacy of objectives have also been considered, and discussion has been devoted to such topics as: the extent to which objectives are unitary, the clarity of an objective's intent, ensuring that performance indicators are part of an examinee's repertoire of behavior, and determining that performances, conditions and standards are specified in operational terms. In criterion-referenced measurement, objectives may be considered inappropriate for any one or more of the following reasons:

- Unclear main intent.

- Improper performance indicators.

- Performances, conditions and standards not specified in operational terms.

- Coverage by an objective of more than one separate task (i.e. compound rather than unitary).

- One or more of an objective's main parts missing.

Precise operational objectives which are derived from an analysis of the activities and behaviors required for performance of a task or job are necessary inputs to the criterion-referenced test development process. Lack of such inputs will result in tests which are at best marginal indicators of examinee performance, or, at worst, invalid.

3

Considerations
in
Planning a Test

The first step in developing a criterion-referenced test is to construct an overall test plan. The necessary inputs to such a plan include a list of skills and knowledges derived from a task analysis and a clearly defined statement of performance objectives for each task. Planning is an important process in constructing reliable and valid criterion-referenced tests. In the planning process, the test author systematically considers various factors that influence the test, and develops methods to establish test items that will adequately measure the required objectives. Aspects of the test planning process include:

- Determination of the extent to which practical constraints may affect the way in which objectives must be tested.

- If such constraints are identified as problems, determination of methods for selection or modification of objectives.

- Planning the types of items, their format, and their level of fidelity (realism).

- Developing a plan for sampling among items and among conditions, if necessary.

- Determination of the appropriate number of items for inclusion included in a given criterion-referenced test and documentation of the test plan.

Once the test plan is complete, the test author can proceed with the actual development of test items. This topic is covered in Chapter 4.

PRACTICAL CONSTRAINTS

Practical constraints are situational or environmental aspects that have an impact on a test. In most cases, practical constraints associated with development of a test item are specified in the statement of conditions for an objective. In some situations, however, this may not be the case and the test author must determine the extent to which practical constraints will have an effect on testing. The assessment of practical constraints involves checking each objective thoroughly to ensure that the objective can actually be administered. Various types of practical constraints might include:

- Available testing time
- Weather conditions
- Geographic restrictions
- Personnel limitations
- Cost limitations
- Equipment and facilities limitations
- Realism in testing
- Other constraints

Practical constraints are often interrelated. Both time and manpower availability, for example, may be major determinants in affecting the cost of a test.

Available Testing Time

Time factors may directly affect criterion-referenced test development practice. Test administration time, for example, may be a constraint which determines whether or not to use a particular test format such as hands-on testing or simulated testing vs. a lower fidelity (and less time-consuming) format such as multiple-choice testing. In various test situations it may be totally impractical to test a given objective in a hands-on fashion within the time that is available.

Examples such as:

- "Prepare a 40-page report on the state of the recent political crisis in Chicago, within three hours."

- "Monitor a simulated air traffic radar display for a period of 28 hours, maintaining sufficient vigilance to detect all three unauthorized aircraft indications during that period."

are both examples of objectives that are not feasible as a direct function of the imposed time constraints. In fact, both examples would probably require too much time to test operationally, and would therefore require modification in order to permit testing in a shorter amount of time. If a given objective or series of objectives that are tested together require more time than is practically available, it may be necessary to select among the objectives for inclusion in the test, or to develop alternatives which consume more reasonable amounts of testing time.

Personnel Limitations

Personnel availability, or lack thereof, also imposes practical constraints on test development. In many testing situations, for example, it is not possible to employ individualized testing formats that require one-on-one monitoring by proctors for each examinee. In such cases, objectives may require modification in order to enable group examinations, such that one proctor might monitor a number of examinees simultaneously. Another example of a situation where personnel considerations might affect testing involves teams or crews that perform a task in an integrated fashion, and where the objectives of interest require testing one team member whose performance is dependent upon the availability and/or adequate performance of other team members. In such a situation, it may not be possible to use all team members in the test in order to test the single team member of interest to the objective. An example of such a situation might involve a three-man crew whose job is to operate a radar reconnaissance plane; however, the objective of interest in test development addresses only the tasks required of the copilot. If the other crew members (i.e. pilot, navigator, radar observer) are not available for use in the testing situation, it may not be possible to conduct an actual hands-on test for the copilot under normal aircraft operating conditions.

Cost Limitations

Another important factor in criterion-referenced test development involves cost considerations in testing. Particularly in situations where hands-on performance measures are required, occasions may arise where prohibitive testing costs occur in actual operational situations. Where complex equipment is involved, for example, it may be necessary to test for simulated performances rather than to require performance on actual equipment, due to cost considerations involved in operating and maintaining the equipment. If situations arise where the cost requirements of testing all objectives in a group are not feasible, selection among objectives on the basis of cost considerations may be necessary.

Equipment and Facilities Limitations

Situations may also arise where required facilities and/or equipment are not available for test administration. Such situations dictate that test items be developed that circumvent the use of those facilities and/or equipment during testing. Testing in the area of antiaircraft missile launching, for example, may effectively be impossible using actual equipment, and must therefore be simulated in order to achieve reasonable testing costs. A second example might involve computer troubleshooting where test plans that require extensive computer down time may be prohibited for cost or security reasons. In situations where facilities and/or equipment limit testing applications, it may be necessary to modify objectives, or to select among objectives in order to comply with situational constraints.

Realism in Testing

Another important constraint that may have an impact upon criterion-referenced test development involves the fidelity, or degree of realism, of a testing situation. It may not be feasible in testing objectives involving medical diagnostics, for example, to actually have patients available whose injuries or illnesses comply with the testing objectives. In such situations it may be necessary to relax the level of realism in testing, and to move toward simulated situations. A similar example, equally as obvious, involves law enforcement and security occurrences that require the ability to disarm bombs. In a testing situation live bombs would never actually be used, therefore the testing conditions would not be as realistic as may be optimally desired.

Other Constraints

Other practical constraints may also be encountered in test development situations. Constraints involving such areas as: ethical considerations, legal considerations, supervisory effectiveness, communications, and logistics may also influence criterion-referenced test development. Recall that in many cases constraints may be interrelated. Constraints involving equipment availability for instance, may also involve cost, or, similarly, legal or ethical considerations may be inextricably related in personnel-related decisions.

Data Sources.   Undoubtedly the best source of information on practical constraints in criterion-referenced measurement is actual knowledge of existing conditions at the testing sites. First-hand observation of such potential problem areas as: facility and equipment availability, personnel availability, and degree of realism, will allow for informed judgments regarding practical testing considerations. A second major source of information is actual conversations with subject matter experts who are knowledgeable about the testing content. Subject matter experts can play a major role in aiding test design to circumvent various test-related constraints.

OBJECTIVE SELECTION

Two general approaches exist for overcoming the effects of practical constraints in a testing situation: selecting among objectives and modifying objectives. A typical problem with modifying objectives is that the original intent of the objective may easily be distorted as a function of the modification. If it is decided to select among objectives, it is important that the examinees not know precisely which objective(s) have been selected for testing. If examinees understand that they may legitimately be tested on any objective (but do not know which one(s) in particular), they must prepare for all objectives.
The tactic of sampling among objectives should not be employed

in situations where critical objectives are involved. In critical cases, all objectives should be tested. For objectives of non-critical nature however, selection may be used to overcome practical constraints imposed by testing situations. It is important to note that a developer should never select among objectives when examinees need to be certified on *all* objectives.

Suppose for example, a criterion-referenced test was developed for use in evaluating a student's ability to distinguish among stages in the duplication process of a living cell. Four phases of cell division exist. These are termed: prophase, metaphase, anaphase and telophase. In each of the four phases of cell division, a variety of observable actions may be discerned. Let us assume that five discernible stages exist within each of the four phases of cell division. Let us assume further that the objective of interest involves testing students on their ability to discriminate among the 20 (five times four) possible stages. If only a few minutes are available for conducting the test, it may not be possible to require that examinees identify each of the 20 stages from a sample of slides showing various stages of cell division. In such a case it may be appropriate to sample among the stages in a fashion that requires that the examinee identify at least one stage from each of the four phases of cell division. If there were only one major phase, it would not be necessary to sample among phases, and the 20 stages could be sampled randomly.

Two important aspects concerning selection among objectives in criterion-referenced test development are random selection and examinee naiveté. These are indicated in Table 3-1.

TABLE 3-1

Two Aspects of Objective Selection

- Objectives to be tested should be *randomly* selected from the population (or strata) of objectives that are available for testing.

- Examinees should be unaware of which specific objectives will be tested.

If a test author chooses to select among objectives, he can guarantee only the extent to which an examinee is able to perform those objectives that are actually tested. If objectives were selected randomly, or randomly within strata (as was the case with the cell division example) and examinees pass the selected objectives in appropriate numbers, then a reasonable assumption can be made that the examinees can actually pass all objectives. To the extent that sam-

pling occurs over a large domain of behaviors, however, this cannot be guaranteed. If sampling is random and each examinee has an equal chance of being tested on any objective, then a statistical case can be made with some degree of confidence, that any examinee can perform all objectives. Nonetheless, if objectives are sampled, the only *guarantee* which can be made concerns performance on the sampled objectives. It is appropriate to document a plan for selecting among objectives in order that, both during and after actual test development, the method will be retrievable.

MODIFYING OBJECTIVES

Certain testing situations may require modification of objectives, rather than selection among them. The extent to which objectives are modified from their original statement, however, will adversely affect the validity of a test. Modification of objectives should be accomplished with extreme care and with adequate consideration of the desired testing outcome. Generally, it is inappropriate to modify the *performances* required by an objective. Performances indicate the actions or tasks to be actually performed in order to accomplish a testing objective. *Conditions* and/or *standards* are better candidates for modification. It may for instance, be appropriate to lengthen or to shorten test times or test limiting conditions in order to comply with practical testing considerations. It may also be appropriate to retreat from use of actual hands-on performance items to the use of simulated items as a function of cost, facility, or equipment constraint considerations. Objectives should not be modified more than is absolutely necessary in order to maintain the integrity of a test item vs. the objective that it is designed to measure. Consider the following example. Assume that an objective states:

- "Given a complete kitchen set-up, the hospital cook examinee will prepare a dinner meal for 250 patients under standard hospital conditions. The meal must be prepared within three hours, and the examinee must follow stated hygienic regulations. The examinee will have a cook apprentice under his supervision. The meal must be rated as satisfactory by three experienced cooks, all of whom have had five years of experience in hospital meal preparation."

Let us assume that a sight inspection of the testing facilities is made,

and that several facts are identified as potential practical constraints:

- Kitchen facilities equivalent to those in a typical hospital are not available.

- An average of 20 students are being trained simultaneously in a hospital cooking curriculum. Testing time available for all students is 12 hours.

- The available budget will not allow for preparation of enough food for 250 people. A meal for 30 persons is, however, within the available budget.

- Three hospital cooks each having five years of experience are not available to judge the food preparation. Only one such individual is available. Several other cooks are available but none have the required experience.

- Only three test administrators are available.

- Only two kitchens are available.

Considering such constraints, it is obvious that the objective must be modified. The major question of interest concerns how to best modify the objective in order that its intent is not violated. Consider the various types of constraints that are operating in this situation and how they affect the overall objective. Facility and equipment constraints appear minor. There are two kitchens available and both appear adequate. Although the kitchens are not actually in hospitals, it is possible to impose a standard hospital situation by regulating the hygienic requirements of the kitchens to meet the standards required by a hospital. It appears that the resulting loss in test fidelity will not be critical.

Personnel constraints do, however, appear serious. Since only three test administrators are available, it may be difficult to determine whether all examinees are actually following the required hygienic procedures. Another problem is that only one cook with the required level of experience is available as a judge. This constraint imposes an additional requirement upon the testing situation. It is possible, however, that the manpower constraint is too rigorous and that the number of available judges is actually adequate to evaluate the performance of the examinees. In such a case, this constraint might be relaxed under the assumption that it will not seriously affect the validity of the test. The objective could easily be modified to relax the experience requirement for judges.

Time considerations nevertheless appear relatively difficult in this

example situation. The number of examinees to be tested and the time available do not appear compatible. In this situation, time constraints are sufficiently severe that they cannot easily be circumvented. Since available testing time is interrelated with other constraints, such as personnel availability, it may be possible to manipulate the personnel situation and to thus help resolve the time issue. Since two hospital kitchens are available, two examinees can be tested simultaneously.

The objective requires that examinees prepare a meal with the assistance of another cook. It appears that this requirement might also be relaxed by allowing an examinee to function either in the role of primary cook or as the apprentice. If the objective were modified appropriately, four people could be tested simultaneously. Additionally, the requirement that the cook prepare a meal for 250 people may be overly stringent. If, for example, a cook could prepare an adequate meal for 30 persons, such a preparation would appear to demonstrate ability to prepare meals for large numbers of people. These revisions would also reduce testing and therefore the time constraint imposed by the objective might also be relaxed.

Thus if the objective is modified appropriately, two person teams could work simultaneously in each of two kitchens. Also it appears feasible that examinees might be tested on the extent to which they can identify and describe recipes appropriate for 250 people in a written or oral fashion, rather than actually preparing a meal for 250 people; a modification that will further cut testing time. Finally, cost considerations may indicate that the large number of meals required by the original objective is prohibitively costly, and that the objective should also be modified for cost reasons.

In a complex situation such as this one, it might be helpful to construct a table of conditions and standards that require modification. Table 3-2 shows an example for the hypothetical test item discussed. Note that Table 3-2 shows both conditions and standards that require change, and why the changes are required. Use of a table such as that shown in Table 3-2, will help test development by clearly identifying the performances, conditions, and standards that require modification in order to comply with constraints dictated by practical considerations. The hypothetical food preparation objective, after modification, might read as follows:

"Given a complete kitchen set-up, the hospital cook examinee will prepare a dinner meal for 30 patients under standard hospital conditions. The meal must be prepared within two hours and the examinee must follow the prescribed hygienic regulations. The examinee will serve as a member of a two-person team, either as chief cook or as an apprentice.

The meal must be rated as satisfactory by one experienced cook. Recipe preparation will be tested in a written format."

TABLE 3-2

Example Table for Summarizing Conditions and Standards That Require Change in an Objective

Conditions and/or Standards That Require Change	Why Changes Are Required	Proposed Changes
250 people	Budget constraints limit preparation to 30 people	1. Modify to 30 people 2. Use a written test for recipe preparation
Three hospital cooks each with five years' experience	Three highly experienced cooks not available	Substitute less experienced cooks on routine aspects of the judging
Supervise one apprentice	Manpower availability	Examinees may also serve as apprentice cooks
Location in actual hospital kitchen	Hospital kitchen not available	Simulate hospital kitchen: impose relevant hygienic requirements on existing facilities
Three-hour time limit	Too many examinees to devote three hours to test each individually	1. Test two at a time for about two hours each (feasible, if meal is for about 30 people) 2. Have one examinee serve as the apprentice cook

---

LEVEL OF FIDELITY AND ITEM FORMAT CONSIDERATIONS

In constructing criterion-referenced tests, as in all other types of test development, questions concerning item format often arise. Such questions involve decisions about appropriate formats for each objective. Hands-on performance items, simulated performance items, essay written items, multiple-choice items, matching items, fill-in-the-blank items, true-false items, recall measures, job simulations, and supervisor ratings are various possible item formats. Virtually any format can be adapted to most testing situations, however guidance as to appropriate item format is often provided by careful consideration of the instructional objectives. The practical considerations under which a test is administered are relevant in determining item format. Time, personnel availability, and number of items included may suggest easily administered formats that require minimal time. In other situations, due to such factors as high costs to establish hands-on testing procedures or to construct simulators, lower fidelity items may be suggested, and item format thereby prescribed. One general guideline based on a suggestion by Edgerton (1974), is that item styles not be mixed in the same test, so as to avoid measuring "test-taking skill" instead of subject matter competence. Item and format generation such as "item forms" (Hively et. al., 1968) are not yet sufficiently researched to warrant standard use.

In considering this issue, the concept of simulation fidelity becomes important. In many testing situations, it is not practical to demand that examinees actually perform the tasks stated in objectives, and it is therefore necessary to retreat to some type of simulation. In such situations, the issue of fidelity arises. The term *fidelity* refers essentially to the degree of realism in testing *vs.* the actual job performance situation. The more a test item resembles the actual job performance of interest, the higher the fidelity of that item. A paper and pencil test item, for instance, would be a low fidelity representation of a task involving welding proficiency. Paper and pencil items, however, may be very high fidelity representations of tasks which actually require paper and pencil manipulation. Computation of the refund due, or of the tax payable on Internal Revenue Service Form 1040 for instance, is itself actually a paper and pencil task.

Fidelity of simulation is a topic area where practical testing considerations have a direct impact upon test development. If for example, it is prohibitively costly to use actual equipment for a maintenance test, and a simulator is employed, fidelity is reduced, unless the simulator is almost identical to the configuration of the actual equipment on the tasks being examined. To the extent that performance required by a simulator approach those required by actual equipment, fidelity loss is minimized. Reading steam pressure on a boiler gauge for example, may not be seriously degraded by requiring an examinee to read steam pressure on a *picture* of a boiler gauge. Other simulations however, may cause major losses in fidelity. For example, if, in the boiler gauge situation, an examinee was required to detect rate of movement in a needle on the gauge, then simulations using still pictures would indeed be of very low fidelity.

Levels of Fidelity

Frederiksen (1962) has proposed a multiple-level classification scheme for simulation fidelity in performance testing. The first category (and lowest fidelity level) is to solicit opinions. This category may, in fact, often miss the major question of interest (i.e. to what extent is opinion about an examinee's behavior a reliable indicator of actual performance?). The second category is administration of attitude scales. This technique, although psychometrically refined via the work of such investigators as Thurstone, Lickert, Guttman, and others, assesses a primarily psychological concept—attitude—that is presumed concommitant with performance. Frederiksen's third category is measurement of knowledge. This category is without doubt the most commonly used method of assessing performance. The technique is considered adequate, however, only if an objective's intent is to produce knowledge (as opposed to actual performance). The fourth category is to elicit "related" behavior. This approach is often used in situations where, due to practical considerations, it is necessary to resort to observations that are thought to be logically related to the behavior required by the performance criterion. The fifth Frederiksen category is to elicit "What I would do" behavior. This technique usually involves presentation of descriptions of problem situations, or scenarios, under simulated conditions, and requires that examinees indicate what they would do to solve the problem, if in the situation. Finally, at the highest fidelity level, Frederiksen suggests elicitation of actual lifelike behavior. This category involves performance assessment under conditions which approach the realism of the real life situation. Table 3-3 shows Frederiksen's scale.

Matching Fidelity Level with the Objective

Obviously, item format and fidelity are closely related. Practical constraints may dictate use of low simulation fidelity formats for cost or for administrative reasons, because such tests may be simple to administer or easy to score. Edgerton (1974) has suggested a good practical guideline for item format. Edgerton suggests that test developers select the format that best approximates the behavior specified by an objective. If an objective concerns problem solving, then items should address problem solving, and not for instance, knowledge about problem solving or knowledge about required background con-

TABLE 3-3

Levels of Simulation Fidelity*

Fidelity Level	Types of Measurement
Low Fidelity	—Opinions
	—Attitudes
	—Knowledge
	—Related Behavior
	—Simulated Behavior
High Fidelity	—Lifelike Behavior

*After Frederiksen, 1962.

tent. If an objective involves evaluation of performance, then the appropriate items should address *evaluating* the performance, not actually *doing* the performance. Item format and test fidelity are difficult issues; however, following Frederiksen's guidelines as shown in Table 3-3, will provide a good basis for selecting the highest fidelity level practicable, consistent with situational constraints.

Another important consideration is that item formats not be widely mixed in a test, so as to avoid measuring "test-taking skill" instead of subject matter competence. As stated previously, it is considerably easier to develop high fidelity performance tests for procedural tasks than for abstract tasks, because procedural tasks generally include objectives that are more easily specified in terms of concrete behaviors.

Consider an example involving determination of an appropriate item format for a testing objective. Assume that an objective requires developing a test whose purpose is to assess the extent to which an examinee can prepare and deliver an appropriate speech on an assigned topic. Assume the objective is as follows:

"Given five hours of research, prepare and deliver a speech on the status of solar energy as a major potential home energy source for the United States. Briefly address the following points: passive solar energy in the home, active solar energy in the home, and the necessity for homeowner conservation in combination with a home solar program."

At issue now is what item format to employ in testing the objective. If a paper and pencil test at a relatively low level of situational fidelity is used the test would not appear to assess adequately the objective of preparing and delivering a speech. Neither would tests about knowledge of solar energy and about speech preparation techniques adequately assess the objective. The best way to adequately address such an objective would be to develop a test item which requires that the examinee actually prepare and deliver a speech on the topic of interest. Depending upon situational constraints, the speech might address only a subset of the topics required in the objective (item sampling), or it might require less preparation time on the part of the student (objective modification). Nonetheless, although the two modified alternatives are somewhat less stringent than the behavior required by the objective, they are both definitely preferable to a paper and pencil test.

OBJECTIVITY OF MEASUREMENT

Each of Frederiksen's categories (shown in Table 3-3) appears to possess both advantages and disadvantages. Optimally, a test author would hope to assess performance at the highest possible level of fidelity. Unfortunately, this may often require subjective measurement techniques. In order to minimize measurement subjectivity it may in some cases be necessary to decrease the level of simulation fidelity in a test, so that more objective measurement (such as for example, time and errors) can be employed. In low fidelity performance testing situations, such as those using paper and pencil, or multiple-choice formats for example, objectivity in scoring is readily apparent. Such tests can be computer scored. In higher fidelity testing situations, it is relatively simple to maximize objectivity in procedural areas such as electronic maintenance performance. In abstract areas such as creativity and leadership, however, objectivity in scoring is considerably more difficult to achieve. To the extent that objective measurement is not achieved, test reliability is diminished. One suggested method for maximizing objectivity in abstract areas is to require multiple scorers to assess each individual. Interrater agreement can then be established. If low interrater agreement is found consistently, a test should be revised.

Paper and pencil items are often considered to be a preferred format alternative in test construction. As discussed previously, paper and pencil items are in fact high fidelity representations of paper and pencil skills. They may be used effectively in such areas as evaluating knowledge, use of information, written computations, and problem-solving exercises. Such items are, however, low fidelity representations of hands-on or of performance skills. Advantages of written test items include ease of scoring and objectivity of measurement, since it is generally easier to score a written item than a hands-on item. Furthermore, scoring can often be accomplished more reliably because the measures are less prone to rating or judgment errors. Written items therefore, are often (relatively) reliable. They measure approximately the same thing virtually every time they are administered. Hands-on (or performance) items, on the other hand, while often less reliable, are often more valid. They are more likely to measure the actual required performances than are written items. A good guideline for employing written items is that they should be used in situations which themselves involve writing, or when practical constraints prevent selecting among objectives.

Several formats are often used in written item construction. These include: multiple choice, matching, completion, true-false, and production items.

Multiple-Choice Items

Multiple-choice items can be easily adapted to various testing formats. The usual format has the standard best answer (but not necessarily the *only* correct answer) included in the test item. A major disadvantage of multiple choice items is versatility. See Denova (1979) for a discussion of multiple-choice (and other paper and pencil type) item construction techniques.

Matching Items

Matching items generally employ two lists of terms, where the examinee's task is to match the items in one list with the appropriate items in a second list. This type of written item is considered appropriate for items involving object recognition and for items addressing low fidelity representations of knowledge components. Such items are not recommended for use in criterion-referenced performance testing.

Completion Items

Completion items typically have two forms. In one, incomplete sentences are provided to an examinee, who is asked to complete the sentence by filling in a blank at its end. The second format is similar, but in this format, each sentence has several blanks. Completion item formats are also not considered generally appropriate for criterion-referenced performance testing situations.

True-False Items

True-false items present a factual statement, and each examinee is asked to determine whether the statement is in fact true or false. In performance testing, such items have a number of disadvantages:

- High scores can often be obtained merely by guessing, since there are only two possible outcomes for each item.

- Often, when such items are presented out or context, it is difficult to determine whether true or false is the correct response.

- In many situations, true-false items are developed from sentences that are extracted verbatim from training material. This is considered disadvantageous because it encourages memorization by the examinee.

A good rule of thumb in performance testing is to avoid true-false items entirely.

Production Items

Production items (often termed *essay* or *oral production* items) typically require that an examinee *create* an answer to a prespecified question. Production items may be disadvantageous in criterion-referenced measurement, due to the subjectivity required to score the item. It may be difficult to operationally define behavioral requirements for an answer that is generated creatively. Additionally, to some extent, this type of item may actually measure test-taking skill, writing skill, or verbal skill as opposed to skill or knowledge in the subject matter area of interest. Thus an examinee may be erroneously scored highly, merely because of superior writing or speaking ability. This confounding of subject matter expertise with production item responses is considered inappropriate in criterion-referenced measurement.

Advantages of Written Tests

Several advantages are nevertheless noted for written-type tests. These include:

- Easy maintenance of efficient records

- Easy and reliable administration

- Coverage of a large quantity of material in a relatively short amount of time

- Easy scoring by machine or by hand

It is often difficult to relate written testing formats to actual job performance requirements. Situations often occur where an examinee may pass a written or an oral test item merely as a function of writing or speaking skill or of knowledge (rather than of performance) capability. If, for example, an examinee passed a written test on knowledge of procedures for conducting open heart surgery, would this ability demonstrate competence to actually perform the surgery? The answer is obviously No. This example demonstrates the generic problem with written testing in assessing job performance. In general, written tests are appropriate for subject matters which require knowledge (instead of performance) competence, or for content areas where the performances required by the task itself are themselves written performances.

PROCESS *Vs.* PRODUCT MEASUREMENT IN CRITERION-REFERENCED TESTING

An important issue in criterion-referenced test development involves the extent to which measurement should be restricted to "right" answers *vs.* measurement of the extent to which the "proper" procedure(s) were performed by an examinee, regardless of the final result of that performance. One way to score troubleshooting problems for example, is to determine whether or not an examinee is able to identify a defective component. Such a method scores only the *product* of troubleshooting. If a product-oriented scoring scheme is used, it is difficult, if not impossible, to determine which of many potential causes may have resulted in a failure to solve a problem. An examinee may have made errors in the use of technical data required for problem solution, or errors may have been made in the use of test equipment, or logical errors may have been committed in deciding where to make the troubleshooting check. Observation of the performance *process* may enable identification of the causes for failure.

Another area of concern in scoring products alone is that there may be only a single task in a given task category. If only the product of that task is scored, only one score is obtained for each subject in the task category. Also, for some tasks, there is no "product" at the end of the "process." Maintenance checkout procedures for example, may include such steps as: energizing the equipment to be checked, making all required checks, and de-energizing the equipment. If performance of a procedure is not measured, it may be impossible to determine whether in fact the process has been accomplished correctly, and this may be a primary item of interest. For an excellent discussion of process *vs.* product scoring, see Osborn (1973).

Deciding on Product or Process Measurement

In a criterion-referenced performance test, an examinee is judged against predetermined criteria. Measurement may involve either product or process scoring. In developing a test plan, it is necessary to determine whether an objective specifies that a process be performed or that a product be achieved. A product generally refers to something which is tangible and which can be readily measured as to presence or absence. A process on the other hand, generally refers to the degree to which an examinee follows procedures correctly, regardless of the outcome of the actions.

As suggested by Osborn, product measurement is always appropriate if an objective specifies a product. Product measurement also appears appropriate in situations where:

- The product can be measured as to either presence or characteristics such as length, wattage, diameter, etc.

- The procedure leading to the product can vary without significantly affecting the product.

Process measurement is indicated in situations where objectives specify that a sequence of activities be observed, and when the performance of these activities is equally as important as the product achieved by their completion. Process measurement is also appropriate, according to Osborn, when products cannot be distinguished from processes, or when a product cannot be measured for reasons of safety or other constraining reasons. Generally, process measurement appears appropriate when:

- Diagnostic information is needed.

- There is no product at the end of the process.

- Additional scores are needed.

- The product always follows from the process.

- High costs or other practical constraints prohibit measurement of a product.

Various situations may also arise in which both process and product measurement are appropriate. Consider for instance, the following situations:

- Process and product are similar in terms of importance but it cannot be assumed that a product will necessarily meet criterion levels merely because a process is followed at criterion levels. (An example of such a situation might be a maintenance checkout procedure, where one error in a process might negatively affect the ultimate product.)

- Situations may arise where, although a product is more important than the processes that lead to its completion, there are critical points in the process which, if misperformed, may cause damage to personnel, facilities, equipment, etc.

In deciding whether to use product or process scoring to assess an objective, the criterion specified in that objective must be followed. If the criterion specifies a process, then process scores should be used to assess its achievement. If on the other hand, product scores are indicated, then product scores should be used. In general, product scores are always preferable to process scores in situations where both may be obtained. Osborn (1973) has suggested three categories of tasks to illustrate the relative roles of process and product measurement:

- Tasks in which the product is itself the process. (Relatively few tasks are of this type. Playing a musical instrument, public speaking, springboard diving, and gymnastic performances are examples.)

- Tasks in which the product always follows the process. Fixed-procedure tasks are of this type. In such tasks, if a process is correctly executed, the product necessarily follows. If, for example, recipes are followed properly, a delicious meal will result.

- Tasks in which the product may follow from the process. A large number of tasks fall into this category, where a process appears to have been correctly carried out, but a product was not necessarily obtained. At least two reasons for such occurrences exist. Either the objective was inaccurate in specifying the necessary and sufficient steps in task performance, or the steps were not accurately measured. Archery competition for example, illustrates that there is no guarantee of acceptable marksmanship, even if all procedures are correctly followed. In such a case, process measurement cannot accurately substitute for product measurement.

Before deciding to employ process measurement in criterion-referenced testing, the following issue should be resolved:

- If a process measure is used, how certain can we be from the process score that the appropriate product or task outcome will be achieved?

If the certainty is marginal, product measurement is definitely preferred.

RATING SCALES

If rating scales are used in criterion-referenced measurement, strict definitions should be specified about the rating required to achieve a performance criterion. A so-called behaviorally anchored rating scale (such as the five-point scale shown in Table 3-4) is recommended for use criterion-referenced measurement situations where ratings are found necessary.

Uses of Rating Scales

Rating scales may be employed before and after a training cycle in order to evaluate training, or to set minimum competency levels. A student may, for example, be required to achieve a "one" in order to enter a course and a "six" to graduate. If a student achieves a "six" upon entry, he may not require instruction. Rating scales can also be used to provide feedback to examinees. If a student is rated continuously throughout an instructional program, the student may be able to pace his achievement according to the ratings.

TABLE 3-4

Example of a Behaviorally Anchored Numerical Rating Scale

Rating	Behavioral Anchor
1	Knows rules of tennis, can bounce ball and hit it over net
2	Hits forehand strokes with consistency, backhand weak
3	Hits both forehand and backhand strokes with consistency
4	Can place ball accurately, including serves, volleys and half volleys
5	All strokes are accurate, firm and consistent, topspin and underspin strokes can be employed as required

Dealing with Rating Error

A general problem with rating scales, even those that are behaviorally anchored, is that judgment is required. Subjectivity influences rating scales, no matter how hard one tries to eliminate it. The more clearly anchored the rated behaviors are, however, the more reliable the resultant ratings will be. If each point on a scale can be behaviorally anchored, increased measurement reliability will result over scales where only the endpoints are anchored or where no anchors exist.

Several methods exist for minimizing rating errors. Since criterion-referenced tests generally require examinees to actually display behaviors (i.e products or processes) they may in many situations depend heavily on observations by the tester. A rater should exercise care in order to rate performances or products under precisely the same conditions for all examinees, using the same scale. If a rating of "four" on a seven-point scale is specified as the standard acceptable for achieving an entry-level criterion, the standard should be exactly the same for all examinees. In such a case, a rating of "four" means that the minimal acceptable standard for entry has been met, and agreement has been previously achieved on what the standard should be.

Four general categories of rating error exist. These are as follows:

- Error of standards

- Error of halo

- Logical error

- Error of central tendency

Error of Standards.   A rating error known as the *error of standards* may occur in situations where an adequate specification of discrete standards against which observers must provide their ratings is not provided. If specific standards are not provided for raters, each rater will impose his own idea of the standards against which he should rate. These internally imposed standards may vary widely. Rating errors may therefore be caused by the lack of specific guidance on standards of performance to be rated. The more precisely rating standards are stated (such as in a behaviorally anchored numerical rating scale), the more reliable the ratings will tend to be. Inter-rater agreement will also be enhanced.

Error of Halo.   In many situations a rater's judgment may be biased by his general impression of the individual being rated. Such bias is known as *halo*. The halo bias may be either positive or negative, but shifts in ratings that can be attributed to overall impression of the examinee by the rater, do in fact cause errors. If an observer is favorably impressed, the shift may be toward the high end of a rating scale; if negatively impressed, the shift may be toward the low end. Unless extreme, the error of halo may often go undetected; it is difficult to identify and even more difficult to overcome. Error of halo can be reduced by behaviorally anchoring each point on the rating scale.

Logical Error.   A logical rating error occurs when a rater gives similar ratings to two independent behaviors on the erroneous assumption that the behaviors are related. It may appear to a rater that two independent behaviors are related when, in fact, they are not. To the extent that a rater's judgment is affected by such considerations, logical error is said to occur. For example, if a rater believes that the concepts of efficiency and productivity are highly related, an individual achieving a high rating on productivity may achieve a high rating on efficiency also, although the high rating on efficiency is undeserved. One way to minimize logical rating errors is to emphasize the distinctions among different issues to be rated. Raters should be informed that separate independent traits are being rated and that the extent to which they may, or may not, be interrelated should be ignored in the ratings. Again, it is recommended that the rating points be behaviorally anchored to the extent possible.

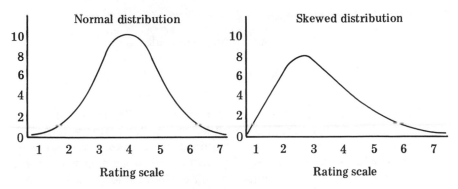

FIGURE 3-1   Normal and Skewed Distributions of Ratings

Error of Central Tendency.   The error of central tendency in rating occurs as a function of the natural tendency of raters to force ratings into a normal distribution. That is, most people will be rated in the middle of a rating scale, with only a few being rated at the extremes. In rating scales with odd numbers of rating categories, for example, one may often observe a large number of ratings at the midpoint, even if the variable being rated is not naturally distributed according to a normal or bell-shaped curve. Figure 3-1 shows a normal (or bell-shaped) rating distribution as compared to a nonnormal (or skewed) distribution for the same seven-point rating scale. The rating error which artificially imposes normality (by assigning most ratings to the central categories on a rating scale) upon distributions which are actually skewed is known as the *error of central tendency*. One way to counter this error is to use rating scales with an even number (i.e. four, six, or eight) of rating categories. Such scales have no identifiable midpoint and therefore tend to reduce the error of central tendency by forcing raters to spread their ratings across the midpoint. Again, however, the best solution is to anchor the rating categories with statements which describe the required performances.

TYPES OF RATING METHODS

Let us now turn to consider several categories of rating methods. Four specific types of performance rating scales are:

- Checklists
- Numerical scales

- Descriptive scales
- Behaviorally anchored numerical scales

Checklists

Checklists are useful methods for rating ability to perform set procedures. Checklists are also a simple way to determine whether or not an examinee has achieved a required performance standard. In situations where checklists are appropriate, performances are typically broken down into elements which are then rated (checked) on a go, no-go basis on the extent to which each item has been successfully performed. Checklists help to reduce the error of standards because they tend to minimize subjectivity. Instead of large numbers of rating categories, from which scorers may choose, only two (go and no-go) exist for each item or element on a checklist. Where possible, checklists are recommended in criterion-referenced performance testing situations over other rating methods. The reason for this recommendation is that checklists tend to be a very reliable form of rating. A checklist for various tasks involved in saddling a horse might for example, look like Table 3-5.

TABLE 3-5

Sample Checklist

Yes	No	Item
		• Is the saddle properly in place on the horse?
		• Is the saddle properly positioned on the saddle pad?
		• Are the stirrups at the proper height for the leg length of the rider?
		• Are the stirrups firmly secured to the saddle?
		• Is the girth strap tightened so that the saddle will not slide?
		• Etc.

Numerical Scales

Numerical scales divide performance into a fixed number of points which are anchored only by numbers. Data suggests that, in most cases, raters can reliably discriminate among at least five perceptual categories, but among no more than nine. This phenomenom is known as "the magical number seven, plus or minus two" (see Miller, 1956). Most numerical rating scales therefore should contain between five and nine points. Table 3-6 shows a numerical rating table.

TABLE 3-6

Sample Numerical Rating Scale

How well does the examinee write programs in Fortran?

1 Very Poorly	2	3	4	5	6	7 Very Well

Descriptive Scales

A descriptive rating scale employs phrases rather than numbers to identify different levels of performance ability. In descriptive rating, obviously, the number of categories can be varied to suit the required performances, making such scales relatively versatile. Disadvantages associated with descriptive scaling include questions as to the interpretation of the phrases. Such ambiguous phrases as "good," "excellent," "many," "poor," and "few" may be interpreted differently by different raters. To the extent a phrase is behaviorally oriented, errors will be reduced. Another disadvantage to the use of descriptive scales concerns the impression of the rater involving the interval among descriptive categories. Many raters for instance, tend to think that "fair" and "poor" are closer together in terms of their interval than are "good" and "excellent." Table 3-7 is an example of a descriptive rating scale.

TABLE 3-7

Example Descriptive Rating Scale

How well does the examinee ski?

Very Poorly	Poor	Average Skill Level	Well	Very Well

Behaviorally Anchored Numerical Scales

Behaviorally anchored numerical scales are those that use both behavioral phrases and numbers to anchor the rating points. Both the numbers and phrases, therefore, are considered by the rater. To the extent that phrases are operational definitions of the categories of the objective to be rated, rather than abstract terms such as poor, fair, good, and excellent, rater bias will be minimized. An example of a behaviorally anchored numerical scale is shown in Table 3-4.

In general, behaviorally anchored numerical scales which rate products will be more reliable, and consequently more valid, than will other types of ratings, including process ratings. This is true since products are usually relatively tangible. If, for example, after completion of a performance test, the product produced is compared to the required product, that comparison may be rated. Such a procedure minimizes rating errors since it provides the rater with a tangible standard against which to compare an examinee's product.

SAMPLING AMONG ITEMS AND CONDITIONS

Another consideration in planning a test is the extent to which it may be necessary to sample either within a specific objective, or among objectives. Sampling within an objective should be considered when there are several legitimate ways to test a given objective. Sampling within objectives is often necessary in situations where the objective deals with abstract concepts. Examples of such situations include:

- Problem solving (being able to diagnose and repair malfunctions in TV circuitry)

- Categorical concept testing (identification of species of animals, categorizing emotional disorders, selecting a suitable floor space layout for an office building)

- Mathematical concepts (addition, multiplication, correlation, factor analysis, probability)

Item sampling often applies in situations involving abstract or conceptual behaviors. Where concepts are being tested, it is generally not possible to develop items that measure all aspects of the concept. Mathematics provides a simple example of this problem. It is not feasible, for instance, to develop test items which measure all possible three-digit number additions. It is therefore necessary to establish a testing situation in which items measuring the objective are selected according to a sampling plan. One might for example, develop five or six items, each of which address certain aspects of the domain to be tested and assume that an examinee who can pass such items could actually achieve mastery in the entire domain, if tested. An important point is that if one concept is very similar to another concept, large numbers of potential items can be created by sampling from both concepts. For example, in developing a criterion-referenced test in the area of aircraft recognition, many of the developed items could be used to assess recognition of general types of aircraft, of both U.S. and of Soviet manufacture.

Osburn (1968) has suggested that when sampling items within an objective, the items should be selected by random sampling from the content universe. Another investigator, Hively (1974), has suggested the use of generalized "item forms" for constructing items in situations where the content domain has large numbers of items from which to sample. An item form is essentially an item development algorithm whose purpose is to ensure that all items addressing a given content domain are constructed similarly (according to the algorithm). In situations where huge numbers of items can be created from a specific content domain, criterion-referenced test developers may wish to consider such an approach. In most performance testing situations, however, it will probably be unnecessary.

At least two factors exist which affect the necessary number of items to be selected when sampling within an objective. One involves the relative importance of correct classification (i.e. whether or not an examinee has mastered the concept). If it is critical that an examinee master a concept or performance (for example, tests to assess proper procedures for sterilizing surgical equipment), additional items should be included in order to ensure that examinees have actually mastered the required performances. The second factor involves limitations imposed by practical constraints. Often, such testing constraints as personnel availability, equipment availability, time, and costs may preclude development of some preferred items.

MULTIPLE CONDITIONS IN
ITEM DEVELOPMENT

Often, criterion-referenced tests must be constructed to assess performance under diverse situational conditions. Ambulance attendants, for example, must be able to administer first aid under virtually any kind of environmental or situational condition (i.e. in a person's bed, in the middle of a busy street, at 100-degree temperatures, in a snow drift). A basic question that must be resolved in test development is:

- Under what conditions should the performance required by the objective be demonstrated?

In situations such as the ambulance attendant example, it may be necessary to limit the number of conditions to be tested as a function of practical considerations. In other situations, however, this may not be the case. For each objective, it is necessary to examine the range of applicable conditions and to sample among them carefully in developing a test. In situations where large numbers of conditions occur, it may be appropriate to rank the conditions in order of importance and to develop items for testing the required performances under each of the conditions ranked in the top 25 percent. Such a technique will ensure that examinees can perform the required performances under a wide array of conditions including the most critical ones.

ESTABLISHING THE NUMBER OF ITEMS
TO INCLUDE IN A TEST

In establishing how many items to include in a test, guidance can be obtained by considering the objective. The more complex an objective (i.e. the more subobjectives it includes), the larger the number of required items. Several additional factors also affect the number of items to include in a test. Among those, two important considerations are:

- The variety of conditions under which each performance should be tested

- The appropriate standard of performance for each objective

The first consideration has been discussed in the preceding pages. Situations may occur, however, where objectives do not specify testing under multiple conditions, but where multiple conditions might nevertheless be applicable. In such situations it is necessary to develop as many items as appear feasible considering the practical constraints in the testing situation. If a relatively specific objective is stated, such as for example,

"Be able to install a Maytag model 213 washing machine."

it may be relatively easy to develop items to test the objective. However, if the actual purpose of the objective was to be able to install *any* home washing machine, a number of additional items may be necessary in order to ensure that an examinee can in fact meet the stated requirements.

A second factor, the level of acceptable performance required by an objective's standards, must also be considered in determining the number of items required for a criterion-referenced test. It is necessary that enough items be included to ensure that the performances required by the objectives are met. If, for example, an objective requires that a chemistry experiment be completed in 20 minutes, and the examinees rush frantically to complete the experiment, it may be appropriate to create several items covering that objective in order to be certain that the examinees achieve mastery. Each item must match the objective to ensure that objectives have been performed to the specified standards. It may be appropriate to require that examinees perform several similar chemistry experiments, all within a specified time limit. In this situation the objective is actually being modified. It is necessary to have a solid, legitimate rationale for modifying objectives. Where such modification does appear necessary, however, the modifications should occur during the test development process, and *not* during test administration.

General guidelines for determining the number of items required to assess an objective suggest that each item must clearly match the stated objective, even if several items are required to test a given objective. Additionally, enough items must be created to ensure that, if passed, the examinee has met the stated standards. It is, however, important to guard against creating large numbers of items that test extremely rare performances under conditions which are difficult to imagine. All required performances, conditions, and standards must be covered by the items. An important point to consider is that the reliability of a test (a topic covered in a later chapter) is influenced by the number of items.

Detailed prescriptions for establishing the precise number of items required to test a specific objective do not exist. In general, it is recommended that as many test items be included as situational and time constraints will permit; however, motivational and fatigue factors may also affect test performance and thus must be considered when establishing the number of items to be included in a test. On this topic, Graham (1974) has indicated that, "Even for highly homogeneous tests, four or five items (per objective) may be necessary to minimize classification errors." This is particularly true in situations where examinees are being selected on the basis of test results, and is true even for tests which measure relatively confined and/or circumscribed domains. For more heterogeneous tests, inclusion of additional test items may be even more critical.

A good rule of thumb is to write considerably more items than are necessary. Leftover items may be used to create alternate or parallel test forms, or to replace items which, upon tryout, appear for one reason or another to be inadequate. A pool of items larger than the number required enables item analyses to be conducted so that only the best items are selected for inclusion in a final criterion-referenced test. (Procedures for item analysis will also be covered in a later chapter of this book.)

DOCUMENTING A TEST PLAN

In discussing test planning, we have mentioned such topics as:

- Item format and level of fidelity

- Overcoming practical constraints, by selecting among or by modifying objectives

- Sampling items within objectives

- Sampling among multiple conditions

- Determining the number of items to include in a test

Table 3-8 shows a sample worksheet format that may be used to help document a test plan. A worksheet such as that shown in Table 3-8 can be constructed for each objective covered in a criterion-referenced test. Table 3-8 shows a sample worksheet format, and Table 3-9 shows the sample worksheet filled in for several hypothetical objectives.

By creating a worksheet such as the one shown in Table 3-8, the information necessary to construct test items and to determine the appropriate number of items is readily available. The entry in the "number of items required" column in Table 3-8 should be the number of items required on the final version of the test. Again, it is

TABLE 3-8

Sample Test Plan Worksheet Topics

Objective	Select Among Objectives?	Format	Fidelity Level	Type of Measurement	Type of Scoring	Sample Among Multiple Conditions?	Sample Items Within the Objective?	Number of Items Required

TABLE 3-9

Hypothetical Example of a Completed Test Plan Worksheet

Objective	Select Among Objectives?	Format	Fidelity Level	Type of Measurement	Type of Scoring	Sample Among Multiple Conditions?	Sample Items Within the Objective?	Number of Items Required
Dig a 20-ft. long ditch, 1-ft. deep in 20 min.	All objectives are to be tested	Hands-on performance	High	Product	Pass-Fail	Only one condition	No—test item is *only* item. Dig a 20-ft. ditch in 20 minutes	1
Correctly install electrical conduit in ditch	All objectives are to be tested	Hands-on performance	High	Process and Product	Pass-Fail (Checklist on both process & product measure)	Only one condition	No—test item is only item. Install electrical conduit	1
Fill in and rake ditch	All objectives are to be tested	Hands-on performance	High	Product	Pass-Fail	No—test both filling in and raking	No—test items only items. Item 1—fill in ditch Item 2—rake ditch	2 Fill in ditch Rake ditch

appropriate to create more items than are necessary, and to then select the final items by review and by item analysis techniques presented in the next chapter of this book. For further guidance in the areas of measuring instructional intent and item writing, refer to Denova (1979).

SUMMARY

In Chapter 3 we have described several of the various requirements involved in planning for a criterion-referenced test. Such practical constraints as available testing time, personnel limitations, cost limitations, equipment and facilities limitations, realism in testing, ethical considerations, legal considerations, supervisory effectiveness, communications, and logistics have been mentioned. Sources for obtaining information on testing constraints have been indicated. We have also discussed the primary methods for overcoming practical constraints in criterion-referenced testing: objective selection and objective modification. In selecting among objectives, two primary considerations are:

- Objectives to be tested should be *randomly* selected from the population or strata of available objectives, and

- Examinees should be unaware of which specific objectives will be tested.

If objectives are to be modified, the effects of practical constraints must be thoroughly considered, and the objective conditions and/or standards which require modification must be operationally identified and modified according to the requirements of the objective(s) in question.

Item format and level of item fidelity are described in a conceptual fashion. Frederiksen's (1962) classification system for levels of fidelity is discussed, and the importance of matching fidelity level against each objective is emphasized. The issue of measurement objectivity is introduced in this chapter, and various item formats such as multiple-choice, matching, completion, true-false and production items are described.

A major discussion is devoted to the issue of process *vs.* product measurement in criterion-referenced testing. Situations where process measurement, product measurement, or both are applicable in criterion-referenced measurement are indicated. Various types of rating scales are described in this chapter, and their uses identified. Rating errors, such as those involving standards, halo, logic, and central tendency are discussed. Such diverse types of rating scales as checklists, numerical scales, descriptive scales, and behaviorally anchored scales are described and their various assets and liabilities mentioned.

Issues which surround the topic of sampling among items and conditions are discussed, and the difficult topic of establishing the number of items to include in a test is raised. Generally speaking, it is recommended that *at least* twice the number of items as will finally be required for a test be initially constructed. A method for developing a test plan worksheet is proposed and an example worksheet is provided.

4

Constructing
an
Item Pool

In criterion-referenced measurement, the process of constructing an item pool requires the development of items that are designed specifically to test the performances specified by their antecedent objectives. The process of matching test items to performance objectives involves a variety of additional issues, all of which are treated in this book. These include:

- Practical constraints in the testing situation
- Test format
- The number of items required to test a given objective
- Test fidelity

Inadequate objectives are useless in establishing criterion-referenced tests. Performance-oriented objectives stated in operational terms are necessary for development of adequate criterion-referenced test items.

Practical constraints that influence a testing situation must be systematically considered prior to constructing test items. Constraints such as tester availability, testing conditions, time considerations, cost, and facility and equipment availability obviously affect test development activities. Consideration of such practical constraints are important aspects in the development of criterion-referenced test items. Such considerations have a direct impact upon the fidelity (degree of realism) of a test.

Good criterion-referenced test items should measure performances at the highest level of fidelity practicable, consistent with situational constraints. In cases where critical performances are tested, it is even more important to develop items whose fidelity levels are sufficiently high to ensure adequate task mastery.

More items than are actually necessary for the planned test should be created in order to allow for selection of the best items for use in the final test. In establishing the test plan, the numbers of items required to test each objective have been established, and the performances, conditions, and standards that each item must address have been determined. In developing the item pool, it is necessary to create enough items to ensure that the specified objectives are covered in their entirety, and that examinees who pass the items will in fact be appropriately classified as masters in the topic area(s) being tested.

THE SIZE OF THE ITEM POOL

It is advisable to create at least twice as many test items as are planned for the final test. Three general reasons exist for creating an item pool of this size. First, some items will undoubtedly be discarded by test reviewers or for practical considerations during the test development process. Second, items may also be rejected by the statistical item analysis techniques described in Chapter 5. These techniques are designed to ensure that test items that discriminate properly between masters and non-masters on the tasks are selected for inclusion in a final criterion-referenced test. Third, in many situations, it is appropriate to create alternate item pools, or even to develop alternate or parallel forms of a criterion-referenced test, in order that simultaneous testing can occur.

If, therefore, a test plan calls for one item, at least two should actually be created. If a plan calls for ten items, 20 or more should be created. If a test plan specifies that an objective requires six items,

three under each of two testing conditions, a total of at least 12 items should be constructed (six or more under each of the two testing conditions).

STEPS IN WRITING CRITERION-REFERENCED ITEMS

The process of creating test items requires a fair amount of creativity and ingenuity. The test plan worksheet discussed in Chapter 3 is a good basis for creating items. The steps in creating criterion-referenced test items are as follows:

1. Consider each objective on the list of objectives to be tested on the worksheet. If all objectives are to be tested, start with the first objective on the list. If sampling among objectives is appropriate, start with the first objective specified for selection by the sampling plan.

2. Consider the alternatives for item format, fidelity level, type of measurement, and type of scoring. All items must meet the required specifications.

3. Consider the worksheet column headed, "Sample items within objective?" This column indicates the extent to which items should be sampled from a large group of appropriate items. If sampling is required, the column should indicate the characteristics that are necessary for each item.

4. Consider the column headed "Sample among multiple conditions?" This column indicates the condition(s) under which each item must be tested. It should specify precisely how many conditions are to be tested and what the conditions are.

5. Look at the column, "Number of items per objective." This column indicates the number of items to be prepared for each objective on the worksheet. Recall that if one item must be tested under each of two conditions, two items—one for each condition—should be created.

6. Actually create the items specified by the worksheet. Create all items specified for each objective under development in the criterion-referenced test. When creating items,

note the performance called for in the objective (whether it is an overt main intent or an indicator). Note also the conditions and standards specified by the objective. Then prepare the items following the test plan specifications, making sure that the performances, conditions, and standards specified by the objective are accurately reflected in the item. Ensure that each test item includes precisely the same conditions and standards (no more, no less) as are specified in the appropriate objective. If sampling among conditions, ensure that the items effectively sample the required conditions.

Consider the following example objective:

"Given all wrenches necessary for washing machine repair, identify the wrench required to replace the fan belt on a model Z32 washing machine by selecting that wrench from among the wrenches provided."

An item developed to test this objective, which required that an examinee select from among all tools in the entire repair shop, would be inappropriate given the conditions specified. Instead, the examinee should be required to select the appropriate wrench for fan belt replacement from among only those wrenches required to repair a model Z32 washing machine. This is the performance required by the objective, and is therefore the performance that should be tested.

In writing items, it is important to ensure that the language in the item is simple. If, for example, an objective requires that an examinee be able to state four basic differences between Theory X and Theory Y management, the item constructed to test that objective should be phrased in a fashion such that the examinee can readily understand the requirement. The item may, for example, indicate, "State four differences between Theory X and Theory Y management," and not, "Evaluate all considerations involving management leadership style and indicate the conditions which discriminate Theory X from Theory Y management in a hypothetical situation."

SELECTING ITEMS FORMATS

Consider a problem involving the development of various item formats for a given objective. An objective reads, "The examinee should indicate the best position for locating a solar collector panel on the roof of the house shown in the enclosed diagram." One possibility in

such a situation is a standard multiple-choice item. Table 4-1 shows such an item.

TABLE 4-1

Example Multiple Choice Item for Solar Collector Location

The best location for the solar collector panel is:

A. On the side of the roof that most nearly faces north.

B. On the side of the roof that most nearly faces south.

C. On the side of the roof that most nearly faces east.

D. On the side of the roof that most nearly faces west.

The item in Table 4-1, however, requires that the examinee demonstrate only a portion of the relevant information for solar panel installation. It is entirely possible that the examinee knows even more precisely the details about solar panel location and that the multiple-choice item does not adequately assess the required behavior. Nor, for that matter is such an item at the highest practicable level of fidelity. In developing an item, it is appropriate to develop the highest fidelity item possible, compatable with the testing situation. For example, Table 4-2 shows an illustrated multiple-choice item which might correspond with the objective in question.

TABLE 4-2

Example of an Illustrated Multiple-Choice Item for Solar Collector Location

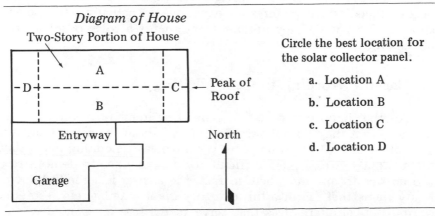

Diagram of House

Two-Story Portion of House

D — A — B — C ← Peak of Roof

Entryway

Garage

North

Circle the best location for the solar collector panel.

a. Location A

b. Location B

c. Location C

d. Location D

A third even better possibility is a simulated performance test item as shown in Table 4-3.

TABLE 4-3

Example of a Simulated Performance Item for Solar Collector Location

---

Place an "X" on the diagram to indicate the best location for installation of a solar collector.

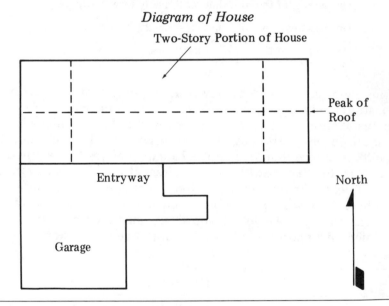

Diagram of House

Two-Story Portion of House

Peak of Roof

Entryway

North

Garage

Finally, at an even higher level of fidelity, a hands-on item might be developed which requires an examinee to actually visit the site and to identify the appropriate location for a solar panel on the house's roof.

Careful Wording in Item Writing

Another important aspect in generating items is to construct the items so that they do not provide "hints" about the correct answer. The other side of the issue, however, involves generating items that do not make it extremely difficult for an examinee to demonstrate the answer to an item when, in fact, the answer is actually known. Many items that fall into this category involve ambiguous, esoteric, or impractical alternatives that serve to confuse an examinee who actually is capable of performing the task required by an objective, but is confused by the ambiguity of the situation.

An example of a written item with a hint might be:

- "A salesman for XYZ Company is entering the office of a potential client. Upon entering, the first thing the salesman should do is to politely:

  a. sit down

  b. greet the client with a firm, sincere handshake

  c. remove his coat

  d. move toward the client's desk."

In this item, grammatical consistency provides a good hint as to the correct alternative. The choice involving greeting the client with a handshake (alternative *b*) is the only listed alternative that can be accomplished "politely." How, for instance, does one "politely" sit down or "politely" take off a coat? The item is inadequate on at least two counts: it provides a grammatical hint, and it is at a very low level at fidelity. Such items should be avoided in criterion-referenced measurement.

INSTRUCTIONS FOR ITEM ADMINISTRATION

Having developed the items for inclusion in a criterion-referenced test, it is necessary to document the technique for item administration. Typically, a test should be designed to include all items of a similar item type (i.e. all multiple-choice items, all hands-on performance items). Thus administration techniques can be generally documented for an entire test (and specifically for each item to the extent necessary). Two general types of situations occur where specific item administration instructions are necessary:

- The item may require that special equipment, facilities, personnel, conditions, standards, or other situational constraints be implemented.

- The item may require that special instructions be presented to the examinee.

Specific item instructions are actually a part of the item and must therefore be included directly with the item. It is inappropriate to adequately develop an item, and then leave the test administrator in confusion as to administration technique. Since the specific instructions for an item are part of the item, an item cannot be evaluated without them. Following are several points that should be considered when developing item instructions:

- Specific instructions should be placed with the item to which they apply. Clear instructions should be indicated as to what part(s) of the items are read by the examinee and what part(s) are read by the administrator.

- The parts of an item which are appropriate only for the administrator should be designated in bold type or should be relegated to a separate test administrator's handbook.

- Specific instructions should indicate clearly the time limits imposed upon each item and should make apparent the extent to which considerations such as speed *vs.* accuracy are more important in item scoring.

- The instructions should provide clear guidance to the administrator in terms of what to do, how to do it, what to say, whether or not to intervene during the item performance, and so forth.

- It is recommended that the adminstrator read the specific instructions for the item verbatim from the administration manual to the examinee.

- Diagrams of equipment and/or facility set-ups should be provided so that confusion and ambiguity are minimized.

- Whenever specific equipment settings such as dial settings and control knob placement are required, these should be unambiguously specified.

- Specific instructions should inform the examinee exactly what performances, conditions, and standards are required.

Instructions may also explain the purpose of various items in a test. For example:

"At this test station you will be tested on your ability to perform certain tasks involving alignment of an optical sight. These tasks will require that you employ the material presented, and align the optical sight on the target reticle to a tolerance limit of plus or minus one degree of arc."

In such a case, the administrator's instructions for that item should indicate precisely what equipment is to be used by the examinee in performing the optical sight alignment task, where the examinee should stand during task performance, and how to instruct the examinee on the performance requirements. A test item is incomplete without the necessary information.

EVALUATING ITEMS

As discussed in detail by Mager (1973), it is important to ensure that all items match their related objectives precisely. Criterion-referenced tests must ensure that the performances, conditions, and standards included in the items match those called out in the appropriate objectives. Item intents (for overt items) or performance indicators (for covert items) must be identified in the objective. The required performances in the item must be the same as those required by the objective. If item and objective performances match in terms and intent, the item should be revised in order to ensure that a one-to-one match occurs. Additionally, it is important to ensure that the standards in each item match precisely the standards required by the objective. Finally, the conditions specified in the test items must match the conditions under which the performance is to be demonstrated, as specified in the objective.

Additional checks on item adequacy include the following:

- Ensure that each item is clear and unambiguous. A criterion-referenced test item must not be susceptible to misinterpretation either by the test administrator or by the examinee.

- Ease of administration: Each item should be designed in a fashion that facilitates administration to the greatest extent possible consistent with the objective. Items complex to administer are subject to the possibility of increased measurement error and decreased item validity. For example, if an item is intended to assess general soldering skills, it would not be appropriate to require an examinee to solder microminiature capacitors and transistors on an electronic circuit board. Such an item would be difficult to administer because it calls for a degree of soldering precision that is greater than is specified in the objective, and because damage to valuable components may occur as a function of the increased specificity of the test item over the skills required by the objective. Instead of employing such a precise example, it would be more appropriate to require that the examinee solder two pieces of wire together on a large chassis. The point is that the item should be practical and easy to administer and should address as precisely as possible the level of specificity called out by the objective (no more, no less).

- Item fidelity: The level of item fidelity must be appropriate for the required objectives. If an objective calls for hands-on performance, the item generated should require hands-on performance, and not a simulation. In general, the higher the level of item fidelity, the more valid the test. A number of technical issues involving physical fidelity *vs.* psychological fidelity arise in this issue, and the interested reader can consult Adams (1979) for further information. In general, however, the higher the fidelity of test items, the more valid the overall test.

- When revising inadequate items, be sure to revise their specific instructions also. This is necessary in order to ensure standardization in item and test administration.

GENERAL INSTRUCTIONS FOR CRITERION-REFERENCED TESTS

Proper instructions are an essential part of any test. The test author must ensure that instructions for test administration are as clear and unambiguous as possible, yet deal with all anticipated contingencies in test administration. Specific instructions for the administration of each test item should be appended directly to the item. Additional instructions are, however, required for administration of the entire test. General test instructions should include the following types of information:

The Purpose of the Test

For example:

- "This is a test of your ability to assemble a ten-speed bicycle gear mechanism."

- "This is a test of your ability to encode a message into a cryptographic code."
- "This is a test of your knowledge of traffic regulations."

Time Limits for the Test

For example:

- "You have 20 minutes to complete this test."
- "You have 15 minutes to complete the first part of the test, 20 minutes to complete the second part, and ten minutes to complete the third part."
- "We expect that this test will take about one hour to complete but no time limit is imposed. If it takes you longer feel free to use all the time you need."

Description of Test Conditions

For example:

- "This is an open book test and you will be allowed to use any sources you may wish."
- "You will be tested while suspended in a tank containing a salt water solution."
- "All tools necessary for performance on this test are provided on the table in front of you."

Description of Test Standards

For example:

- "The number of items missed on this test will be subtracted from the number of items correctly answered."
- "You will be scored on your ability to follow the precise steps specified in the checkout procedure."
- "In order to receive credit you must get the exact answer for each item."

- "You will be rated on the clarity of your presentation."

Description of Test Items

For example:

- "Circle the letter showing the correct choice—*a*, *b*, *c*, or *d*."
- "For each problem, record your calculations to the third decimal place and round off to two decimal places."
- "Identify the proper form for reporting an error in your time sheet and indicate the error on the sample time sheet provided."

General Test Regulations

For example:

- "Raise your hand if you need assistance."
- "As soon as you have finished the test you may leave."
- "Do not talk to anyone during the administration of this test. Talking will cause you to fail the test."

SUMMARY

Chapter 4 has discussed various techniques for constructing a pool of items for use in criterion-referenced testing. If a test plan calls for one item for use in assessing an objective, *at least* two such items should be created.

Six steps appropriate for the creation of criterion-referenced test items are listed. In abbreviated form, these are:

1. Consider each objective on the test plan worksheet.

2. Consider available alternatives for item format, fidelity level, type of measurement, and type of scoring.

3. Determine whether sampling within objectives is appropriate.

4. Establish whether sampling among conditions is appropriate.

5. Determine the required number of items to create.

6. Create the required items.

A discussion dealing with the topic of item format selection is presented and several techniques and instructions for administering items are discussed. The issues of item evaluation, in terms of ambiguity, ease of administration, fidelity and item instructions, are raised; and general instructions for criterion-referenced tests are considered. Such general instructions should address at least the following topics:

- The purpose of the test
- Time limits
- Testing conditions
- Test standards
- Test items
- General test regulations

5

Selecting
Final Test Items

In preceding chapters, we have discussed issues involved in the construction of criterion-referenced test items, and techniques for ensuring that each item is compatible with the objective upon which it is based. In this chapter, a method is presented for constructing a test from the pool of items previously developed, in a way designed to ensure that the test is able to discriminate between people who are known to have the skills required by the objectives (masters) and people who do not (non-masters). Good items are those which discriminate between known masters of the test content and known non-masters. In addition, good items are those which do not confuse examinees and which are known to cover the necessary content domain.

The number of items developed for a given criterion-referenced test should be considerably larger than the actual number required for the final test. Developing such an item pool allows for items to be selected for use in the final test on a tryout basis rather than on the basis of opinion. In selecting final items for inclusion in a test, the test developer should have available a pool of about twice as many items as are required for the final version of the test. It is also necessary that all relevant objectives be covered by a test. In situations where objectives refer to a specific content domain (i.e. multiplication), for example, test items should sample from that domain. In situations where objectives refer to specific task performance, test items should address the performances, conditions, and standards specified. At least one item should be included in the final test which measures each relevant objective. In many cases, it is appropriate to have multiple items for a given objective. It is also important to ensure that all items selected for tryout directly match the performances, conditions, and standards specified in the relevant objective, are clear and unambiguous, are within the repertoire of behavior of the examinee, are constructed at the appropriate level of measurement fidelity, are relatively simple to administer, and adequately cover the subject matter content prescribed by the objective.

Even after such a thoughtful consideration of each item, an empirical tryout of the items should be conducted. This chapter describes procedures for trying out an item pool and for selecting final items for inclusion in a criterion-referenced test. The end product is a final version of a criterion-referenced test ready for validation.

TRYOUT TECHNIQUES

Selecting a Tryout Sample

The population of individuals used to try out a criterion-referenced test consists of two distinct classes of persons. Those who are known to be masters in the subject matter content that the test was developed to assess, and those who are known novices (i.e non-masters) in that subject matter content. About half the tryout sample people should be composed of masters and the other half, non-masters. This requirement exists because the major premise of the item analysis technique recommended in this book is that acceptable items are able to reliably discriminate between subject matter masters and non-masters. If a test is being developed to assess the content of a training curriculum, the master portion of the tryout sample should be people who have already passed the course segment that the item pool addresses, or who are otherwise known to be competent in the subject matter area, such as for example, instructors. The other half of the tryout sample should be composed of people known to be naive. They may, for instance, be persons who are enrolled in a training program but who have not yet encountered the portion of the curriculum that the test purports to examine.

Thus, about half the tryout sample may be expected to achieve "go" or "pass" scores on the items in the test whereas the other half of the sample may be expected to receive "no-go" or "fail" scores. If, for example, a test is designed to assess the competence of experienced intelligence analysts, the master portion of the tryout sample subjects might be composed of experienced intelligence analysts who are known to be competent. The other half might be composed of "new hires" or others who have yet to become involved in intelligence analysis. If the subject matter area of interest concerned intelligence estimates of the Soviet Union, the master half of the tryout sample might be experienced Soviet analysts whereas the non-master half might be analysts who have no expertise in Soviet affairs. A good guideline is to administer the item pool to the same type of people as those who will take the final version of the test. Half the people in the tryout population should be masters, and half should be non-masters. If a test will be administered to several different groups, the items on the test would be tried out on individuals from each of these groups. Again, half the sample should be composed of known subject matter masters and the other half, non-masters.

Sample Size

The number of individuals to be included in a tryout sample is based upon two primary considerations:

- The number of items in the item pool
- The size of the population for whom the test is intended

Including too many subjects in a tryout sample is rarely a problem. The difficulty generally lies in finding enough subjects to aid in trying out test items. The number of items in the item pool is the most critical factor in determining a tryout sample size. A general rule is:

- Have at least 50 percent more people in the tryout sample than items in the item pool. For example, if there are 100 items in the item pool, with the expectation of finally developing a 50-item test, there should be 150 subjects in the tryout sample. Of the 150 subjects, 75 should be content area masters and 75 non-masters.

If possible, an even larger tryout sample than the 50 percent increase over the number of test items is recommended. The greater the proportion of people in the sample to items in the item pool, the more likely it is that the item analysis results will be reliable.

A second factor to consider in determining tryout sample size is the size of the population for whom the test is intended. The basic principle here is:

- The tryout sample size should be proportionately related to the size of the population for whom the test is intended.

In other words, the larger the size of the population for which a test is intended, the larger should be the tryout sample. In order to be representative, a tryout sample should have enough people to reflect the composition of the population to which the test is intended to generalize. That is, if a test is intended primarily for Hispanics, or for policemen, then the tryout sample should be composed primarily of Hispanics, or of policemen, respectively. There are no set rules for determining sample size relative to the size of the test population, but Table 5-1 provides some guidelines.

TABLE 5-1

Guidelines for Tryout Sample Size

Size of Population to whom Test will be Administered	Tryout Sample Size
20 or fewer	8 to 12
50	15 to 20
75	20 to 25
100	25 to 30
200	40 to 50
500	70 to 80
1,000 (or more)	80 to 110 (or more)

As can be seen from Table 5-1, if the population for whom the test is intended is relatively small, the tryout sample size can also be small. As the population size increases, however, the tryout sample size must also increase proportionately. Recall, however, that there are two considerations in determining tryout sample size: the size of the population to which the test is intended to generalize, and the number of items in the test. For small populations, the determination about sample size will generally be made by the number of test items. Of the two factors, number of items in the test is the most critical. Thus, it is not appropriate to use fewer than 50 percent more people than items, even if tryout sample size could be smaller based on population size.

A third important point in establishing a test tryout sample is:

- The tryout sample must be selected randomly.

Random selection in this case means that the persons included in the tryout sample should be chosen at random from the population of people to whom the test is intended to generalize. The persons actually included in tryout samples should therefore be selected by chance. A random sample provides the best sample representation of the entire test population. There are a variety of ways of constructing random samples, and most statistics books contain in the appendix a table of random numbers which may be used for this purpose.

One simple way of constructing a random sample is to obtain lists of the two appropriate types of people (masters and non-masters) available for the tryout. Write the names of the masters on separate slips of paper and place the slips in a container. Shuffle the slips thoroughly and without looking, pull the slips out of the container. When as many slips as are needed for the sample of masters have been selected, discard the other names and repeat the process for the non-masters. Such a process ensures accurate construction of a random sample of the master and non-master populations.

In a training situation, another way of constructing a tryout sample might be to administer the test to a randomly selected group of incoming trainees (prior to their having completed a curriculum segment). If this group is tested before training they may be considered an accurate sample of non-masters. Submitting the same test to a randomly-selected group of individuals who have completed the training segment would provide a similar sample of masters. In such a case, it is important that the two groups (the pretest group and the posttest group) be independent (i.e. composed of different persons), as a systematic bias will occur if the same group is tested twice, both before and after training).

An Illustrative Problem in Determining a Test Tryout Sample

Consider a test having five items, which is to be employed in a course having 50 students. How many people should be included in the test tryout? Assume students in a current training program are being used to develop a test for a forthcoming program.

Consider the following parameters:

- A test having 5 items should have at least 10 items in the tryout pool.

- An item pool of 10 items requires that 15 persons be included in the tryout.

- A population of 50 persons in the course indicates a tryout sample of approximately 15 to 20 persons.

- Both masters and non-masters are required.

In such a case, it would be appropriate to randomly select a total tryout sample size of 16 persons, and to administer the 10-item pool to 8 persons prior to training (i.e. non-masters), and to the remaining 8 persons following completion of the training program (i.e. masters). Such a procedure will provide for an adequate tryout sample.

Following are several conditions which should be established when trying out an item pool:

- It is helpful to inform the subjects in the tryout sample that they are being included in the process of developing a test. Subjects can be instructed to note ambiguities or problems with the items from their point of view and to report them.

- The same general test instructions and specific item instructions that will be used in the final form of the test should be employed in the tryout. (This may not always be possible because of revision of instructions or of items on the basis of the tryout.) Try to match the tryout instructions as closely as possible to those that will occur in the final test.

- Use the tryout to evaluate both general test instructions and item instructions. Make notes as to where ambiguities or unclarities occur and revise the instructions as appropriate for the final version of the test. All tryout subjects should receive the same instructions in order to increase test standardization.

- It is important to ensure that the test measures knowledge and skill in the subject areas covered, rather than understanding of test instructions. Test instructions should be as unambiguous as possible.

- Testing conditions should be as close to those anticipated in the final version of the test as possible. Optimally, they should be identical. Short cuts in applying conditions in the test tryout will invalidate the items and prohibit reasonable determinations about subject matter mastery. For example, if a test allows a manager trainee to spend two hours in the preparation of a plan for transporting 20 computer terminals to Europe, the tryout should also allow two hours to prepare the plan, as opposed to short cutting to half an hour. Similarly, if a test requires outdoor administration, administer it outdoors during tryout also.

- Each item should be administered exactly as will be done in the test itself. If this requires that two test administrators be available to administer the final form of a test, two administrators should be available for the tryout.

- Test standards should be the same in the tryout as they are for the final version of the test, and scoring the results of the tryout should occur exactly as they will in the final test administration. In general, the tryout should be considered exactly as though it were the final version of the test and it should be administered as such.

PERFORMING AN ITEM ANALYSIS

Traditional item analysis techniques, like other statistical techniques developed for norm-referenced measurement models, have limited application in criterion-referenced measurement due to restricted score variance in criterion-referenced tests. Although several promising recent studies have suggested techniques for increasing the variance of criterion-referenced test scores (Haladyna, 1974; Woodson, 1974) many such techniques are still experimental (see Berk, 1980). Until additional research develops and refines approaches to item analysis that are appropriate for criterion-referenced measurement models, an index which relies on the use of subject matter masters and non-masters appears appropriate. Basically, masters and non-masters are tested, and their pass-fail patterns on various items are recorded. A statistical coefficient known as ϕ(phi) is then computed using fourfold tables (i.e. master, non-master vs. pass, fail) for each item. Acceptable items are those which are passed by masters and failed by non-masters. An item is considered poor if there is little difference between the numbers of masters and non-masters who passed or failed the item. If more non-masters than masters pass an item, the item is considered unacceptable. Items receiving low ϕ coefficients thus, often must either be discarded or carefully reconsidered prior to inclusion in a criterion-referenced test.

Use of the phi coefficient is a widely accepted item analysis technique. Four types of data are necessary:

1. We need to know what people who fail an item were previously classified as masters.

2. We need to know what people who fail an item were previously classified as non-masters.

3. We need to know what people who passed an item were previously classified as masters.

4. We need to know what people who passed an item were previously classified as non-masters.

Given these four types of data, we will be able to compute a ϕ value for each item in the tryout item pool.

Calculating ϕ[1]

Consider an example of calculating ϕ. Assume we plan to have a four-item criterion-referenced test. An item pool consisting of eight items is thus constructed, and a proper tryout subject sample consisting of 12 persons (12 is 50 percent more than the number of items, and the population for which the test is intended is fairly small) is obtained. Table 5-2 shows the results of the tryout.

---

[1] The ϕ statistic has been selected for use in this book as the technique of choice in conducting item analysis, as well as for estimating test reliability and validity (see Chapter 7) for two primary reasons. First, while many more sophisticated techniques exist for such purposes, the attempt in this book is to present a simple, practical technique for estimating these parameters in the hope that increased use will result. Second, as compared to other simple four-fold techniques (i.e. tetrachloric r, x^2, biserial, and point biserial r, etc.) ϕ is considered either to be more appropriate from the perspective of naturally dichotomous data, or more conservative since it can approach unity only when the marginal totals are equal. The ϕ statistic, therefore, will produce a slightly lower correlation estimate than will the comparable tetrachloric statistic, for example. This conservatism is viewed as the appropriate direction for error in criterion-referenced item statistic determination and in test reliability and validity estimation. For additional information on these and similar issues, refer to Guilford (1965), pp. 317-319 and to McNemar (1962), pp. 197-198.

TABLE 5-2

Example Item Tryout Results[1]

Examinee	Category	*Test Item Number*								Number of Items Passed
		1	2	3	4	5	6	7	8	
1	Masters	P	P	P	P	P	P	P	P	8
2		P	P	P	P	P	F	F	P	6
3		P	F	P	P	F	P	P	P	6
4		P	P	F	P	P	F	P	F	5
5		P	F	P	P	F	P	P	P	6
6		F	P	P	P	P	F	F	F	4
7	Non-masters	P	P	F	P	P	F	P	P	6
8		F	P	P	F	F	F	P	P	4
9		P	F	P	F	F	F	F	F	2
10		F	F	F	P	P	F	P	F	3
11		P	F	F	P	F	P	F	F	3
12		F	F	P	F	F	F	F	F	1
Number Passed—Masters		5	4	5	6	4	3	4	4	35
Number Passed— Non-masters		3	2	3	3	2	1	3	2	19
Total Number Passed		8	6	8	9	6	4	7	6	54

*P = pass   F = fail

[1] Adapted from Swezey and Pearlstein (1975).

In Table 5-2, half the subjects included in the tryout sample are masters (i.e. individuals who have already demonstrated competence in the subject matter) and the other half, non-masters (i.e. individuals who are not knowledgeable in the subject). From the tryout data shown in Table 5-2 consider item five. In order to compute a ϕ coefficient for item five, we require:

- The number of masters who gave the correct answer to item five.

- The number of masters who gave an incorrect answer to item five.

- The number of non-masters who gave a correct answer to item five.

The number of non-masters who gave an incorrect answer to item five.

Table 5-3 shows a matrix for organizing the data in order to simplify the computation of ϕ. The matrix shows the appropriate data for item five. In the top-right margin of the matrix is shown the totals of Cell A plus Cell B (i.e. the total number of masters in the tryout sample). Similarly, the lower-right margin (C + D) shows the total number of non-masters. The bottom left-hand margin (B + D) shows how many people failed the item, and the bottom right-hand margin (A + C) shows the total number of people passing the item. The marginal totals, from both the right-hand side and from the bottom of the table, equal the total number of people in the tryout sample for item five. It is important to set up the matrix for computing ϕ exactly as is shown in Table 5-3. The ϕ technique will not work properly if the matrix is constructed differently.

TABLE 5-3

Sample Matrix for Computing a ϕ Coefficient for Item Five

Results on Item Five			
	Fail	Pass	
Masters	B 2	A 4	A+B = 6
Non-masters	D 4	C 2	C+D = 6
	B+D 6	A+C 6	Σ 12

Table 5-4 shows item matrices filled out with the tryout results for each item shown in Table 5-2. Compare Table 5-2 to Table 5-4 in order to see how the matrices were established.

The formula for computing ϕ is shown in Eq. (5-1).

$$\phi = \frac{(AD)-(BC)}{\sqrt{(A + B)\,(C + D)\,(A + C)\,(B + D)}} \qquad (5\text{-}1)$$

Formula for Computation of ϕ

The numerator of the ϕ formula equals the value of Cell A multiplied by the value of Cell D, minus the value of Cell B multiplied by

TABLE 5-4

Example Item Matrices for the Eight Items Shown in Table 5-2 [1]

Item No. 1	Fail	Pass	
Masters	B 1	A 5	A+B 6
Non-Masters	D 3	C 3	C+D 6
	B+D 4	A+C 8	12

Item No. 2	Fail	Pass	
Masters	B 2	A 4	A+B 6
Non-Masters	D 4	C 2	C+D 6
	B+D 6	A+C 6	12

Item No. 3	Fail	Pass	
Masters	B 1	A 5	A+B 6
Non-Masters	D 3	C 3	C+D 6
	B+D 4	A+C 8	12

Item No. 4	Fail	Pass	
Masters	B 0	A 6	A+B 6
Non-Masters	D 3	C 3	C+D 6
	B+D 3	A+C 9	12

Item No. 5	Fail	Pass	
Masters	B 2	A 4	A+B 6
Non-Masters	D 4	C 2	C+D 6
	B+D 6	A+C 6	12

Item No. 6	Fail	Pass	
Masters	B 3	A 3	A+B 6
Non-Masters	D 5	C 1	C+D 6
	B+D 8	A+C 4	12

Item No. 7	Fail	Pass	
Masters	B 2	A 4	A+B 6
Non-Masters	D 3	C 3	C+D 6
	B+D 5	A+C 7	12

Item No. 8	Fail	Pass	
Masters	B 2	A 4	A+B 6
Non-Masters	D 4	C 2	C+D 6
	B+D 6	A+C 6	12

[1] Adapted from Swezey and Pearlstein (1975).

the value of Cell C. The denominator is the square root of the multiplied marginal totals. In order to compute the final ϕ value, the numerator is then divided by the denominator.

Consider a sample calculation of ϕ using the data for item two in Table 5-2. Looking at item two, we obtain the following values:

$$
\begin{aligned}
A &= 4 \\
B &= 2 \\
C &= 2 \\
D &= 4 \qquad \textit{Data for item 2 in Table 5-2}\\
A + B &= 6 \\
A + C &= 6 \\
B + D &= 6 \\
C + D &= 6
\end{aligned}
$$

Total sample size = 12

Substituting these values into Eq. (5-1), we obtain:

$$
\begin{aligned}
\phi &= \frac{(4 \times 4)-(2 \times 2)}{\sqrt{(6)\,(6)\ \ (6)\,(6)}} \qquad\qquad (5\text{-}2)\\
&= \frac{12}{\sqrt{1,296}} \\
&= \frac{12}{36} \\
&= .33
\end{aligned}
$$

Computation of ϕ for item 2 in Table 5-2

Similarly, substituting in Eq. (5-1) using the data in item 4, we obtain:

$$
\begin{aligned}
\phi &= \frac{(6 \times 3)-(0 \times 3)}{\sqrt{(6)\,(6)\ \ (9)\,(3)}} \qquad\qquad (5\text{-}3)\\
&= \frac{18}{\sqrt{972}} \\
&= \frac{18}{31} \\
&= .58
\end{aligned}
$$

Computation of ϕ for item 4 in Table 5-2

Use of the ϕ Coefficient

ϕ is a special case of a Pearson product moment correlation coefficient, for use with dichotomous variables. Its values may range between a negative 1.00 through 0 to a positive 1.00. Table 5-5 shows the range of values for ϕ.

TABLE 5-5

Range of Values for ϕ[1]

Values of ϕ may fall anywhere along this continuum.

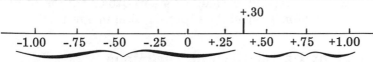

+.30

| -1.00 | -.75 | -.50 | -.25 | 0 | +.25 | +.50 | +.75 | +1.00 |

Unacceptable or Doubtful Item Values   Acceptable Item Values

[1] Adapted from Swezey and Pearlstein, (1975).

The ϕ values for all eight items shown in Table 5-2 (and in Table 5-4) are presented in Table 5-6.

TABLE 5-6

Values of ϕ for Items in Tables 5-2 and 5-4[1]

Item #	ϕ
1	.35
2	.33
3	.35
4	.58
5	.33
6	.35
7	.17
8	.33

[1] Adapted from Swezey and Pearlstein (1975).

If the ϕ value of an item is less than +.30, or is negative, the item may be a poor one. Regard values ranging from +.30 to –1.00 as unacceptable or doubtful values which indicate that something may well be wrong with that item. A ϕ value of less than +.30 means that the item does not discriminate well between masters and non-masters. That is, too many non-masters passed the item, whereas too many masters failed it. A negative ϕ value (for example –.35) indicates that non-masters generally did better on the item than masters did. The values of ϕ for the eight items shown in Table 5-6 suggest that item 4 shows the best discrimination between masters and non-masters, followed in order by items 1, 3, 6 (equally) and then 2, 5, and 8 (also equally). Item 7 appears to be a relatively poor item. Review such items closely before including them in the final version of a test. Always consider any item having a ϕ value ranging between -1.00 and +.30 with extreme caution. Items having ϕ values falling in this category are dubious at best, and will probably require some kind of revision or change before they can be included in the final version of a criterion-referenced test. A ϕ value of greater than +.30 indicates that the item is a legitimate candidate for inclusion in a test.

Summary of Use of the Phi Technique

1. ϕ is appropriate for items which are dichotomously scored (i.e. "go," "no-go"; acceptable, unacceptable; pass, fail; or 1, 0).

2. There must be approximately the same number of persons in the masters and non-masters groups for the ϕ statistic to be used appropriately.

3. To compute ϕ for an item, determine four values:

   • How many masters passed the item

   • How many masters failed the item

   • How many non-masters passed the item

   • How many non-masters failed the item

4. Record the information established in step 3, into a two-by-two matrix as shown in Table 5-3, and add the column and row totals. Then compute the grand total, and check it against the number of subjects employed in the tryout. Table 5-7 shows a blank ϕ matrix.

TABLE 5-7

Matrix for Computing ϕ

	Item Results		
	Fail	Pass	
Masters	B	A	A+B
	D	C	C+D
Non-masters	B+D	A+C	Σ

5. Calculate ϕ by substituting the values in the matrix into Eq. (5-4).

$$\phi = \frac{AD-BC}{\sqrt{(A+B)\,(C+D)\,(A+C)\,(B+D)}} \qquad (5\text{-}4)$$

Formula for Computation of ϕ

6. If the value of ϕ for an item ranges between –1.00 and +.30 consider this value unacceptable (or, at best, doubtful) and revise or carefully reconsider the item before including it in the final version of the criterion-referenced test. Such an item does not discriminate well between masters and non-masters. It is often better to throw such items out and to develop new items, rather than to try to modify or to resurrect a poor item.

Additional Aspects of Item Analysis

Use of the ϕ coefficient is the recommended technique for conducting item analyses on criterion-referenced test items, in situations when the items are scored dichotomously (i.e. pass, fail; "go", "no-go"; etc.). ϕ may also be used in situations where test items are given point values (such as on a seven-point behaviorally anchored rating scale). In such situations an arbitrary cut-off point must be established in order to set a pass-fail (i.e. dichotomous) score for each item. The method of establishing criterion-referenced tests presented in this book strongly recommends that a pass-fail score be established for each item. In most cases this will be relatively easy; in a few specialized situations (where ratings occur, for example) the pass-fail score must be determined by the test author on the basis of practical considerations. A variety of other statistical measures exist that are acceptable for other types of scoring arrangements. These may be found in any standard statistical text. See, for example, Guilford, (1965).

The ϕ technique described here is the technique of choice for item analysis in most criterion-referenced situations. There may, however, be a few cases where ϕ is not appropriate. This occurs in situations where very small sample sizes exist (i.e. less than eight people). In such situations, ϕ is generally inappropriate, and a more simple, subjective technique for conducting item analysis is necessary. Due to its inherent subjectivity this technique is considerably less accurate than the ϕ technique.

Item Analysis by Inspection of the Tryout Data

If less than eight observations exist for a given item, the ϕ statistic is not considered appropriate for item analysis of criterion-referenced test items. In such a case, a simple comparison of the number of masters vs. non-masters who passed an item may be conducted. A rough judgment about item selection may be made on the basis of these two numbers relative to each other. Consider the data previously presented in Table 5-2, for example. Although more than eight item observations are shown, we may still use the data to describe the appropriate procedure for small tryout sample sizes. In reviewing the data in Table 5-2, the best item appeared to be item 4. Six masters and three non-masters achieved the correct answer on that item. Items 1 and 3 also appeared satisfactory. Five out of six masters passed these items, while three out of six non-masters passed the items. Items 2, 5 and 8 appeared to be the next best items. These items were marginal, however, with only four out of the six masters passing the items. Among these three items, the best choice would be the item which best rounds out the coverage of the objectives required for a test. Items 6 and 7 appeared to be poor. Only three masters answered item 6 correctly. This item should probably be revised to allow more masters to pass the item. Possibly an unusual or ambiguous word, phrase, or action in that item caused the difficulty. Or possibly the specified performances are not within the normal repertoire of the individual examinee. In such a case, it may be necessary to create a new item in order to resolve that issue. Finally, item 7 showed very little discrimination between masters and non-masters; and so is considered generally poor.

Comparing the results of this analysis of the items by inspection with the results of the ϕ analyses presented in Table 5-6, it can be seen that the results by inspection correspond quite closely with the empirical results. But remember the ϕ technique is always preferred and should be employed where feasible. Use the inspection method only if there are eight or fewer subjects in the tryout sample (i.e. less than four masters and four non-masters).

Cautions in Conducting Item Analysis

A number of cautions should be invoked when considering item analysis results in criterion-referenced measurement. These include:

- Item analyses using the ϕ technique can provide information regarding which items may be inappropriate for inclusion in a criterion-referenced test. The technique does not, however, indicate which items are necessarily *good*. A low or negative ϕ does not mean that an item should be eliminated, but merely that it should be considered carefully before inclusion in a criterion-referenced test.

- The appropriate analytic technique should be employed in criterion-referenced item analysis. ϕ is the technique of choice unless the tryout sample size is very small.

- Certain items may be linked together on a test. That is, they all may be required in order to demonstrate competence on a particular performance objective. For example, a criterion-referenced test involving a performance objective which requires completion of a checkout procedure for starting an engine may have 20 steps in the procedure, each of which can be treated as an item and scored dichotomously. Each step must be completed in turn in order for all other steps to be accomplished. But if all items in the checkout procedure are relatively difficult to perform, with the exception of steps 5 and 6, which are considered to be very easy, an item analysis may indicate that items 5 and 6 have a very low ϕ value (possibly around zero). In this case, items 5 and 6 would not discriminate well between masters and non-masters. In such a case the items could not be discarded, because they are integral components of the overall checkout procedure, all of which is required to meet the performance objective. Whenever items are linked together, it will not be possible to discard the items merely because they have low or negative ϕ coefficients. Either all items must be retained or all must be discarded.

REVIEWING REMAINING TEST ITEMS

We have thus far discussed only one method for reviewing items in an item pool—the use of an item analysis technique consisting of a ϕ coefficient (or inspection) to analyze items regarding their ability to discriminate between known masters in the subject matter area and known non-masters. Since item analysis is merely an aid for use in making judgments about the acceptability of items, it is also appropriate to consider various other ways to judge item acceptability.

Presumably, an item pool containing about twice as many items as required for the final version of a test has been created, and the goal is to select the best items for inclusion in the final version of a criterion-referenced test. It is not necessary to reject half the items in an item pool, since remaining items may be used to form alternate versions of a test. There are several additional ways that items can be reviewed for possible inclusion in a criterion-referenced test. All are essentially subjective. They include:

- Feedback from participants in the tryout sample

- Formal review by independent test evaluation experts

- Formal review by subject matter experts

Feedback from Tryout Sample Participants

The individuals included in a tryout sample can provide valuable feedback in terms of the overall adequacy of test items—their lack of clarity of communication, content, performance difficulties, and problems with conditions and standards. When obtaining feedback from participants in a tryout sample, it is important to emphasize that honest feedback will actually help improve the test. The purpose of the tryout is not to test or evaluate the individuals who partici- pated, but merely to help develop a better test. This must be made apparent to the participants in order to obtain valid and constructive feedback. Table 5-8 shows several questions for use in obtaining item feedback from tryout sample participants.

The question in Table 5-8, "Was the time allowed adequate?" is not relevant if the item has a completion time criterion or a produc- tion rating standard. Such a question is intended for use with items that do not have a specified time standard. If many individuals (say, more than 20 percent of the sample) indicate difficulties with a given item, that item may be a poor one and is a definite candidate for revision or rejection. Following are several points which should be considered in final item selection:

- Are the general test administration instructions clear?

- Are the instructions for administration of specific items clear?

- Note questions asked by tryout participants. These may in- dicate legitimate sources of ambiguity and are extremely useful in revising test items.

TABLE 5-8

Example Questions for Obtaining Feedback on Items from Tryout Sample Participants

Questions (for use with each item in the tryout)

- Were the instructions clear?
- Was the time allowed adequate?
- Was the scoring technique clear?
- Were appropriate equipment and facilities provided?

Other General Questions

- Were the general test instructions adequate?
- Please describe any difficulties or comments.

- Note problems with facilities or equipment. Faulty equipment and/or inadequate facilities may render an otherwise excellent test item meaningless. Consider carefully facilities and/or equipment limitations when constructing a final test.

- If different performance measures are administered at different test stations, note the extent to which bottlenecks occur and redesign the testing situation to eliminate them.

- Note the behavior of the test administrator. Is the test administrator able to observe each examinee accurately on each item? Note also the extent to which the test administrator might inadvertently provide hints while administering various items.

- If examinees make errors, determine whether the errors involve lack of actual subject matter competence or result from such inappropriate issues as: inadequate constraints in the testing situation; specified behaviors which are outside of the examinees' normal repertoire; ambiguity in terms of required performance. A record of observations can be used in diagnosing poor items. Such observations may well be equally as important as the empirical data obtained from the item analysis. It is also recommended that several administrators score each examinee independently, if possible. In this way ambiguities or inconsistencies with each test item can be identified and resolved.

Review by Independent Test Evaluation Experts

A second important class of item evaluation involves review of tryout results by independent test development and/or evaluation experts in order to obtain additional opinions on appropriate items for inclusion in the final version of a criterion-referenced test. Often, such independent experts will be able to point out previously undetected problems with various test items. Such experts are also knowledgeable about item analysis techniques and may be able to aid in interpretation of ϕ coefficient results. These individuals should be provided with complete data on the objectives used to develop the items in order for them to be able to exercise informed judgment.

Review by Subject Matter Experts

A third method of item evaluation is to obtain a content review of each item by subject matter experts. This simple task often greatly facilitates test development by eliminating invalid or ambiguous items. Subject matter experts are a major source of information in criterion-referenced test development, and should be consulted closely in determining the final forms of tests and in item pool reduction. Subject matter experts will help to ensure the accuracy of item content. They can also point out confusing or misleading items. Subject matter experts should, of course, be provided with a list of the objectives upon which the test items are based.

REDUCING THE ITEM POOL

Having completed an item analysis and item pool review, both by test development and by subject matter experts, the next step in the process of developing criterion-referenced tests is to reduce the item pool and to use the remaining items to construct a final version of the test. The final test should incorporate the best items from the item pool. Table 5-9 shows a simple way to summarize item findings. In the "Item Analysis Results" column, items whose ϕ value ranges from –1.00 to +.30 might be indicated. In the "Tryout Feedback Results" column, items where a significant portion of the tryout sample

(20 percent or more) had difficulty might be noted. Similarly items that independent test experts and/or subject matter experts consider poor may also be identified in the appropriate columns.

TABLE 5-9

Sample Item Analysis Summary Table[1]

Item #	Item Analysis Results	Tryout Feedback Results	Independent Test Expert Review Results	Subject Matter Expert Review Results
1				
2				
3				
4				
etc.				

[1] Adapted from Swezey and Pearlstein (1975).

Table 5-10 shows a sample item analysis summary table filled out for a hypothetical item pool containing ten items. Notice that items 1, 3, and 4 appear to be acceptable (i.e. have no checks or other notations). Neither the item analysis, the tryout feedback, nor any form of item review found fault with these items. Item 6 had a low ϕ value but since no other form of review found fault with this item it may well be appropriate for inclusion in the final version of the test. In this hypothetical case, item 7 is shown as inappropriate on all forms of item review except tryout feedback. Such an item should probably be discarded. Item 2 in Table 5-10 might be suspect from the perspective of faulty structure since both the item analysis and the test expert review found it to be unsatisfactory, and since it appeared to have confused people in the tryout sample. Possibly coverage of the subject matter was appropriate in item 2. Item 5, on the other hand, may have demonstrated faulty content but acceptable structure. It appears in this hypothetical example, that items 1, 3, 4, and 6 might be appropriate for the final version of the test with no major revisions. Items 2 and 7 may require major revisions in order to render them acceptable.

The item analysis summary sheet shown in Table 5-10 is merely an aid to help in selecting items to include in the final version of a criterion-referenced test. Judgment obviously plays a major role and,

TABLE 5-10

Sample Item Analysis Summary Results[1]

Item #	Item Analysis Results	Tryout Feedback Results	Independent Test Expert Review Results	Subject Matter Expert Review Results
1				
2	✓	✓	✓	
3				
4				
5		✓		✓
6	✓			
7	✓		✓	✓

[1] Adapted from Swezey and Pearlstein (1975).

since the test author is more familiar with the items than any other person is, use of an item summary sheet may help in establishing informed judgments about which items should be included with no changes, which items might be revised, and which items should probably be rejected out of hand for the final version of a criterion-referenced test.

What to Do if Too Few or if Too Many Items Are Eliminated

Situations may occur in which the item pool has not been sufficiently reduced, or where more than 50 percent of the items in the item pool have been eliminated. If too few items have been eliminaed, no major problem exists. A large number of items, which appear adequate on the basis of various criteria, have been generated. A choice now exists. Either additional items may be eliminated on the basis of personal preference, or an alternative item pool, and possibly an alternative test, may be created. If items are eliminated by personal preference, the original test plan must be followed closely. For example, a 15-item test having three objectives and five items per objective was originally planned. After reducing the item pool, 25 items remain for use in developing the final version of the criterion-referenced test. It will be necessary to ensure that five items per objective still remain, after discarding the extraneous items. If it is decided to use the additional items to create an alternate version of the test, recall that alternate forms may share some items in common; therefore, some items which are included in Form 1, may also be included in Form 2 of a test. It is not necessary that alternate test forms be entirely independent. It *is* important that examinees not be aware of which items are included in which test forms.

Table 5-11 shows 15 possible alternate forms for a test having four items, as constructed from a six-item pool. Note that all 15 forms of the test have at least one item which is different from any other form. Each form, however, has at least 50 percent of its items in common with any other form. Each form, therefore, should be equally suitable as the final version of a test. If sufficient items existed, it would be possible to create alternate test forms with no overlap. Such alternate tests are called *parallel test forms* in psychometric terminology.

TABLE 5-11

Possible Alternate Forms of a Four-Item Test Constructed from Six Items[1]

Forms

Item #	1	2	3	4	5	6	7	8	9	10	11	12	13	14	15
1	✓	✓	✓	✓	✓	✓	✓	✓	✓	✓					
2	✓	✓	✓	✓	✓	✓					✓	✓	✓	✓	
3	✓	✓	✓				✓	✓	✓		✓	✓	✓		✓
4	✓			✓	✓		✓	✓		✓	✓	✓		✓	✓
5		✓		✓		✓	✓		✓	✓	✓		✓	✓	✓
6			✓		✓	✓		✓	✓	✓		✓	✓	✓	✓

[1] Adapted from Swezey and Pearlstein (1975).

If too many items have been eliminated from an item pool, so that the final version of a test does not have the number of items specified in the test plan, new items must be generated. This can be accomplished by following the procedures previously described for creating items for the original item pool. In such a case, the entire item analysis and evaluation process must be repeated using a new tryout sample, including both the good items from the first tryout, plus the new items. If this is not feasible, the minimum acceptable process is to completely try out all new items on the original sample of subjects. New item analysis values and subject matter expert reviews of the new items may then be obtained, and the item evaluation process repeated.

SUMMARY

In Chapter 5, the topic of selecting final items from the item pool is discussed. It is recommended that items be tried out using both known masters of the subject matter content, and individuals who are known to be naive (i.e. non-masters). The number of individuals to be included in the tryout sample is based upon two primary considerations: the number of items in the item pool and the size of the population for whom the test is intended. In general, rules for establishing tryout sample size require that at least 50 percent more people should be included in the tryout sample than there are items in the item pool; and that the tryout sample size should be proportionately related to the size of the population for whom the test is intended. Guidelines for proportionality are indicated. Additionally, it is important that the tryout sample be selected randomly from the population. Examples of tryout sample selection are also presented.

Next, the topic of item analysis is introduced, and a simple four-fold item analysis technique which compares masters against non-masters in terms of pass-fail scores on each item is advocated. The technique makes use of the statistical technique known as phi (ϕ). Numerous examples of the ϕ calculation for item analysis are presented and guidelines for accepting or rejecting items are provided. Items having ϕ coefficients below +.30 are generally considered either unacceptable or doubtful.

Less sophisticated, inspection-based item analysis techniques for items having data on fewer than eight observations are discussed, and an example of item analysis by inspection is provided. It is recommended that such techniques as feedback from participants in the tryout sample, formal review by independent test evaluation experts, and formal review by subject matter experts be considered in evaluating criterion-referenced test items.

Finally, techniques for item pool reduction are provided, and a discussion of what to do if too few or too many items are eliminated from the item pool, is presented.

6

Administering and Scoring Criterion-Referenced Tests

In Chapter 6, various techniques for administering and scoring criterion-referenced tests are discussed. It is imperative that efficient and objective methods of testing and accurate and fair scoring methods be employed in criterion-referenced measurement.

CONSISTENCY IN TEST ADMINISTRATION

The premise of criterion-referenced measurement involves the comparison of performance against an absolute standard, rather than against a distribution of scores achieved by other examinees. Regardless of the lack of emphasis on examinee standings, however, it is important in criterion-referenced measurement (as in all testing situations) to minimize interaction among examinees during testing, unless the objective specifically calls for cooperation among two or more examinees in a group, crew, or team performance situation. It is necessary in administering a test to ensure that examinees have no opportunity to help, hinder, or to observe other examinees during test administration.

Whether the actual test administration is conducted individually or in groups, standardized administration conditions must be maintained. All examinees should have the same opportunity to participate in the testing in exactly the same fashion on each test item. Differences in administration conditions will result in unfairness to some examinees. It is also necessary for test administrators to standardize their own behavior in order not to provide clues to examinees about various aspects of the tests.

Controlling Environmental Variables

When administering criterion-referenced tests, environmental variables that may be presumed to affect test performance should be tightly controlled. Differences among test scenarios in terms of conditions such as lighting, background noise level, temperature, or other items that might affect performance must be standardized for all examinees. If, for example, a test involves auditory acuity, then ambient noise level must be the same for all examinees in order to avoid biasing the test results. Conditions such as heat and humidity can also affect test performance, especially for tests requiring prolonged effort and concentration. Comparable groups tested under comfortable 72-degree temperatures at a reasonable humidity level can be expected to perform better than examinees performing under similar conditions at 25 or at 98 degrees. In general, testing conditions should be stated in the test directions. It is important to standardize environmental conditions in order to avoid bias in testing.

Controlling Personal Variables

Examinees should also be tested under conditions that provide for similar levels of stress. It is entirely inappropriate to test one group of examinees under normal conditions, and another group under high stress conditions. Although a great deal of individual variance can be expected in terms of tolerance to stress (particularly with regard to test-taking anxiety) the test administrator should attempt to control these and other similar interpersonal variables to the fullest extent possible. Such factors as food satiation or deprivation, level of strenuous physical activity, and illness, must be taken into account in testing situations. The situation should be as nearly identical for all examinees as is possible.

Instructions and Tester Variables

Instructions to examinees must be uniform in order to ensure that all examinees are treated fairly. Differences in instructions may provide cues and/or helpful hints to some examinees. In order to avoid such situations, general test instructions, as well as instructions on specific objectives or items, must remain constant across the examinee population. The responsibility for standardization of test

TABLE 6-1

Example Test Instructions

Objective	Instructions	Mode
1. Demonstrate use of a sand wedge.	"For this portion of the test you must hit five balls from the sand trap using a sand wedge. All balls must come to rest on the green, within 20 feet of the hole."	Oral
2. Demonstrate ability to physically move from Rosslyn to Farragut Square on the Washington, D.C. Metro (subway).	"For this aspect of the test you will be provided with a five-dollar bill, and must enter the Washington, D.C., Metro (subway) at the Rosslyn station, buy a fare card, ride the subway to the Farragut Square station, and provide the correct change to the five-dollar bill you were given. You will have one hour to complete this test."	Oral
3. Demonstrate an ability to comprehend written Russian by reading Russian prose passages and answering questions conconcerning the passages.	"In your test booklet you will find three passages from Russian novels. Read each passage carefully, then answer the multiple-choice questions following them. You may go back and reread parts of a passage if necessary. You have 30 minutes to complete this test."	Written

administration conditions rests with the test administrator. Test administrators should be both experienced and capable, and must understand the issues involved in test bias. Contamination of test results as a function of experimenter-induced variables must be minimized. Table 6-1 provides an example of typical test instructions that might be employed in the development of a criterion-referenced test.

Most hands-on performance objectives are product oriented. As has been discussed previously, this is generally considered advisable over process scoring, however, process information may also be collected, should the opportunity arise, even where product scoring methods are indicated. Process information is particularly useful for diagnostic purposes and for evaluation of instructional programs. In the case of linked behavior situations which result in a product, but involve the performance of a process to reach that product for example, errors committed during the process of performing the task may serve a useful diagnostic purpose. It is always appropriate to collect process information to provide tangential data to a product score. If an objective specifies that a product be achieved, however, the examinee should be scored on the extent to which he achieved that

---

TABLE 6-2

Typical Steps in Test Administration

Familiarization
- Read over both the instructions and the complete test.
- If possible observe a similar test being administered by another tester.

Conditions and Materials
- Check testing conditions against those specified and adjust as necessary.
- Assemble necessary test materials.

Admission and Briefing of Examinees
- Check that the work area is comparable for each subject, that all necessary materials are present, and that examinees understand what is required of them.

Instructions
- Read instructions to examinees.
- Begin administration of test.

Process Observations
- Observe examinees' individual performance styles.
- Ensure adherence to standard procedures.

---

product and not the extent to which he performed the process leading to the product correctly. Table 6-2 shows some typical steps which will help ensure standardization of administrative behavior.

It is important to ensure standardization in all aspects of the test situation. Table 6-3 summarizes several components of a test situation that require standardization.

TABLE 6-3

Test Situation Components that Require Standardization

Environmental Variables
- Lighting
- Heat
- Noise
- Temperature
- Humidity
- Etc.

Subject Variables
- Health
- Familiarity with equipment and procedures
- Level of stress
- Visual acuity
- Etc.

Instructional and Administrative Variables
- Availability of facilities and equipment
- Clarity of instructions
- Similarity of conditions for all examinees
- Etc.

SCORING TECHNIQUES

The reason for scoring tests is to obtain an accurate estimate of an examinee's competence. Scoring is often relatively easy in the case of procedural tasks where performance of specified objectives can be directly observed. Either an examinee can replace a broken capacitor or he can not. Either he can accurately set a broken bone or he can not. In cases involving abstract or conceptual tasks, however, assessing performance may be considerably more difficult. Here scoring procedures may tend to move toward the types of rating techniques described earlier in this book. Generally, the more a performance test resembles a hands-on application, the easier it will be to score. To the extent that ratings or other more subjective scoring methods are used, it is recommended that several raters rate the performance and that indices of interrater agreement be computed. In situations where raters do not agree among themselves as to examinee competence (as might be the case in judging springboard diving) the item may not be sufficiently operationally or behaviorally stated (i.e. the error of standards may occur), and may require revision in order to ensure higher interrater agreement.

Scoring Objectivity

Objectivity in scoring should be maximized during the test construction process. In low fidelity tests, those using a multiple-choice format for example, scoring objectivity is apparent (such tests can be computer scored). In higher fidelity tests however, decisions must often be made about scoring objectivity. In abstract task areas (such as ballet dancing and leadership), it may be somewhat difficult to develop objective test-scoring procedures. It is for this reason that rating scales have been historically used as the primary method of assessing abstract tasks. To the extent that objectivity in scoring is reduced, however, test reliability may be diminished. It is appropriate to specify testing objectives as precisely and operationally as possible in order that appropriate items (with associated objective scoring procedures) can be developed. Even in the best of circumstances abstract tests will probably have less objective scoring methods than will tests involving more concrete, procedural task areas. A typical method for maximizing scoring objectivity in abstract testing areas involves use of several scorers to assess each examinee's performance. Interscorer reliability indices may then be computed that will facilitate decisions about mastery.

A number of different types of criterion-referenced test scoring techniques are available. The proper scoring method must be chosen with respect to the objectives under evaluation.

Assist *Vs.* Noninterference Scoring

In criterion-referenced measurement, test items are often constructed such that examinees may perform the entire item without interference by a test administrator. Such a scoring method is termed *non-interference* scoring. In other situations it may be appropriate to allow the test administrator to assist an examinee, that is, to correct the examinee when an error is made, and to allow the examinee to proceed on the basis of the correction. This method of scoring is termed *assist* scoring.

If non-interference scoring is used, score distortions may result in testing situations where inexperienced examinees are tested. In some cases, it may even be impossible to find out how much of a task an examinee can perform, since many subtasks may require proper performance of previous steps. In such a situation, if a test administrator does not in some way assist the examinee, it may be impossible to administer the test, even though the examinee may be able to perform all remaining aspects of a task. The intervention of an administrator does indeed introduce distortion into the meaning of a test score. A slightly distorted score, however, is preferable to no score at all in most assessment situations. If assists are minimized, total score distortion is likely to be relatively minor. Properly controlled, an assist approach to scoring can often be used effectively. The nature of many activities is such that an assist method, which allows the examiner to focus on appropriate remedial steps for improving examinee overall performance, may be necessary. Thus assist methods of scoring are often used in situations where diagnostic information is needed. Focusing remedial training on missed activities may considerably reduce training time and expense where the alternative would be to retrain on all task activities.

Example of an Assist Method of Scoring. Consider a situation in which a clerical examinee is asked to type a manuscript. The examinee may make mistakes during the performance of such a task. But allowing the examinee to proceed even though errors have been made may result in savings of valuable training time. If, for instance, the clerical examinee sets typewriter margins inaccurately, allowing the person to continue even though the margins were set inaccurately, may indicate that additional remedial training is required merely in setting margins, and not, for example, in punctuation, spacing, capitalization, etc.

Pass-Fail Scoring

In general, a dichotomous, or pass-fail scoring technique is recommended for use in most criterion-referenced measurement situations. On most performance tests, examinees should be able to be scored either pass or fail for each item. There are, as has been discussed previously, exceptions to this rule, but in the vast majority of cases, the statement will hold. In pass-fail scoring the examinee either performs the item to the standard specified by the objective or he does not. The item is essentially an observable expression of the standard required by the objective under evaluation, thus performance on the item either meets the standard or it does not; there is no gray area. Consider the following examples:

- An examinee is given ten minutes to detect and replace a faulty transistor in a television set. The examinee either is able to perform this diagnosis, repair, and replacement operation correctly in ten minutes, or not. The examinee is thus scored pass or fail, as appropriate.

- A surgeon is either able to completely excise a tumor or he is not. If an item is generated around a surgeon's ability to completely excise a tumor, and a portion of the tumor remains, the surgeon has failed. Either the tumor is removed or it is not; there is no middle ground. Since a situation such as excision of a tumor involves many steps, all of which must be performed in sequence and correctly, a pass or fail could also be attached to any step in the process. The ultimate pass-fail criterion, however, is whether or not the tumor is removed. (In such a situation, pass-fail scores could be attached both to the steps in the process of removing the tumor, and to the overall criterion of whether or not the tumor was completely removed, as desired.)

Fixed Point Scoring

A second scoring technique employed in criterion-referenced measurement is termed *fixed point* scoring. Fixed point scoring is appropriate when a task or product can be broken down into various levels which can be distinguished quantitatively. For example, an item may call for adjusting precision scale calipers to specified tolerance levels, and if an examinee adjusts the calipers to the exact tolerance levels specified, he may achieve, say, four points; if the adjustment is made to within ±.001 inch, three points; ±.002 inch, 2 points; ±.003 inch, 1 point; and no points would be awarded if the adjustment is off by ±.004 of an inch or more.

Often, fixed scoring techniques may employ pass-fail scoring on each component of a task. Each component successfully performed might be scored pass, or awarded one point. If there are six components to a task, total point score of six would be required in order to achieve a "pass" score on the entire task item.

Consider, for example, the activities required in cooking a steak over charcoal. First the charcoal must be placed in the outdoor grill; second, it must be lit and must burn until all coals are glowing red; third, the steak must be placed at the right height above the charcoal; fourth, the flames from the fire should not be allowed to singe the steak; fifth, the steak must be turned over when one side is cooked properly; and sixth, the entire steak must be removed when it reaches a criterion of medium-rare preparedness (i.e. browned on the outside but red on the inside). As is evident, each intermediate step associated with the performance of cooking a steak might be scored on a pass-fail basis, and then the scores cumulated to obtain a total item score for the item of grilling a charcoal steak.

In the case of fixed point techniques, scoring is often accomplished by using a checklist. All behaviors or products required by the objectives are clearly defined. If the objective involves a product, then scoring may compare the examinee's product to the standard. If, for example, an objective requires filling, sanding, and painting a dented metal surface, each finished product (the painted surface) may be rated by comparing it to a standard surface. The top standard is a smooth, high-gloss metal surface. If the examinee produces such a surface, four points may be awarded. The next level might be a smooth high-gloss metal surface with slight ripples. If an examinee's product resembles this surface, three points would be awarded, and similarly down the scale, where a zero-point standard is represented by a metal surface that is finished so poorly that no points can be awarded.

Multiple Scoring Techniques

Many criterion-referenced measurement applications require that multiple scoring techniques be combined in a single test. These are situations in which pass-fail, fixed point scales, ratings, etc., may be combined in order to assess examinee competence. For example, the task of a Communication Engineer who must be able to maintain all communications equipment within a communications center may involve ability to maintain, troubleshoot, and repair defective equipment, as well as such operational tasks as: receive incoming messages in code, decode messages, transmit messages in code, supervise center employees, etc. In such a situation we may choose to test the maintenance and troubleshooting tasks with "go"-"no-go," or pass-fail items, whereas the encoding tasks may be scored on a rating scale, and ability to send and to receive messages may be scored on a fixed point assignment basis, etc. If items involving similar task aspects of a total job can be grouped together, a criterion-referenced test can be developed to adequately test all relevant job requirements.

Rating Techniques

Rating scales have been discussed in Chapter 3, and include such categories as: numerical scales, descriptive scales, behaviorally anchored scales, and checklists. Recall that a major problem with rating scales involves ambiguity. For this reason, rating scales should be described as objectively and anchored as behaviorally, as possible. Preferred types of rating scales in criterion-referenced measurement include behaviorally anchored rating scales and checklists. Both of these types of scales are relatively amenable to "go"-"no-go," or pass-fail scoring. In order to minimize rating errors in situations where rating scales are employed as the major index of examinee performance, it is recommended that multiple raters assess each item and that estimates of interrater agreement be established.

In order to obtain a rough estimate of interrater agreement, a technique such as the one presented in Table 6-4 is suggested. In this example, a six-item test has been administered to six examinees, and each item has been scored by three raters using a five-point rating scale. Across the rows, scores assigned to each examinee by different raters may be compared. In the sample data shown, it can be seen that perfect agreement among raters exists on items 1 and 5. Some disagreement exists on items 2, 3, and 6, and on item 4, interrater agreement is very low. In this example, item 4 would either have to be revised to increase interrater agreement or be dropped from the test. This is an example of assessing interrater agreement "by inspection," which is a relatively unreliable technique. If, in the development of criterion-referenced tests, one is in a situation where rating scales are being employed frequently, and which involves some difficulty of measurement, the reader is referred the vast body of literature on rating scale development, validation, and computation of empirical indices of interrater reliability. This literature is not treated here, because it is recommended that a dichotomous, pass-fail score be established on every item in a criterion-referenced test. In those few situations where it is not possible to impose a pass-fail scoring system (even by arbitrarily setting a passing criterion on a rating scale, if necessary) the reader is referred to the literature on psychometric development. See, for example, J. P. Guilford's classic *Psychometric Methods* (1954).

TABLE 6-4

Comparisons of Ratings on a Six-Item Test[1]

Item #	Examinee 1			Examinee 2			Examinee 3		
	R_1^*	R_2^*	R_3^*	R_1	R_2	R_3	R_1	R_2	R_3
1	5	5	5	3	3	3	4	4	4
2	5	4	4	4	4	4	3	4	3
3	5	4	5	4	3	3	3	3	3
4	3	5	2	3	1	4	2	4	3
5	4	4	4	4	4	4	3	3	3
6	4	4	3	3	2	3	4	3	4

Item #	Examinee 4			Examinee 5			Examinee 6		
	R_1	R_2	R_3	R_1	R_2	R_3	R_1	R_2	R_3
1	2	2	2	5	5	5	1	1	1
2	1	2	2	4	5	5	2	3	2
3	3	2	2	4	4	4	1	1	2
4	1	2	4	4	2	5	2	3	1
5	2	2	2	4	4	4	2	2	2
6	3	2	2	3	3	3	2	1	2

*R_1 = Rater 1, R_2 = Rater 2, R_3 = Rater 3

[1] Adapted from Swezey and Pearlstein (1975).

In developing rating scales, point assignments must be tied to the criterion levels specified in the objective upon which the item was based. Where possible, point assignments should be behaviorally anchored. Whatever technique is employed, however, rating scales are clearly subjective methods of measurement, and should be avoided to the extent possible. Even worse are situations where rating scales are not anchored. Unanchored ratings are generally inappropriate in criterion-referenced measurement applications.

Establishing Pass-Fail Criteria

If a test measures more than one objective, and if it is therefore necessary to establish a pass-fail criterion, pass-fail cut-off scores should be established for each objective under examination. For example, if one objective on a test has eight associated pass-fail items, a cut-off point for that objective might be set at passing six of the eight items. On a second objective, a cut-off point might be set at passing three of four items. On a two-objective test such as this example, a maximum of 12 possible points exist; however, a total score of nine would not necessarily achieve the requirements for passing, since a requirement exists to pass both six of the first eight items, and three out of the final four items. Thus, it is possible to achieve a total of nine points without having met the criterion on either objective. Establishing cut-off points for pass-fail criteria is a difficult matter. Practical considerations, manpower needs, scoring feasibility, and objective criticality must all be considered in establishing reasonable cut-off scores. In general, cut-off scoring is appropriate when task mastery is feasible, but when factors other than examinee competence, such as carelessness, environmental conditions, and measurement errors may affect a test score; or when a requirement for absolute mastery of a task is not feasible, but an acceptable level of mastery is specified in the objective upon which the test item is based.

Cut-off levels in scoring should be designed to reflect mastery; however, in some cases practical considerations may dictate that cut-off levels be set below 100 percent mastery (i.e. factors other than ability to perform a task, such as careless errors and measurement errors may affect an examinee's test score). If, for example, an objective involves assessment of ability to multiply two three-digit numbers, a typical performance criterion might require ten such sets of multiplication within five minutes, with the examinee achieving the correct answer in at least eight sets. In such a case, the cut-off score of eight (a score of below eight is failing; a score of eight or above is passing) reflects an arbitrary definition of mastery. True mastery requires ten out of ten.

Graham (1974) has suggested that a cut-off point should discriminate masters from non-masters, but as item domains become broad, more heterogenous sets of items are often required, increasing the confounding influence of skills and knowledges that are not directly related to mastery of objectives. For tests measuring objectives having broad domains (or several objectives with different domains) the overlap between true mastery and non-mastery consequently widens. When little overlap occurs between mastery and non-mastery (as is the case for tests measuring a single objective with a relatively restricted domain) setting cut-off scores is less critical. In such a case, the cut-off point should reflect the standard specified by the objective, and can do so without falling into the zone of overlap between master and non-master, since this zone is either narrow or non-existent. On the other hand, if the overlap is wide, the point at which a cut-off score is set is critical. When cut-off scores are set arbitrarily, some misclassification between masters and non-masters will necessarily occur.

False Positives and False Negatives

As mentioned, the basis of the overall criterion-referenced measurement model is that masters be distinguished from non-masters in terms of performance on test items. It is therefore important that classification errors be minimized (i.e. that true masters actually pass the test, and that true non-masters actually fail it). Table 6-5 shows examples of a misclassification and defines *false positive* and *false negative* in terms of their classification error meaning.

TABLE 6-5

Types of Classification Errors[1]

Definition	Possible Reasons for Error
False Positive An examinee is awarded a pass score or a point score above the cut-off, but has not actually demonstrated mastery.	• Measurement error • Bias • Lucky guessing • Cheating • Selective preparation—test just "hit" the right items
False Negative A competent person who has in fact mastered a task is given a failing score.	• Measurement error • Bias • Illness • Unknown behavioral fluctuations • Complexity of instructions

[1] Adapted from Swezey and Pearlstein (1975).

Consequences of either type of classification error may be extremely costly. Incorrectly classifying non-masters as masters (a false positive) can be extremely serious, particularly in situations where subject matter competence is critical. An incompetent individual in a highly critical job may seriously affect the performance of an organization, or the health or well-being of a person in situations where incompetence on a critical task occurs.

A false negative occurs when an individual who is actually a task master is incorrectly classified as a non-master. In general, costs of false negatives, as compared with those of false positives, are relatively low. Nevertheless, huge wastes of money, manpower, and time may occur by incorrectly classifying competent individuals as non-masters.

If the cost of a false positive (incorrectly passing an incompetent individual) is very high, the cut-off point for test scoring should also be set very high. Such an approach will effectively eliminate many examinees who are fairly competent but who are not in fact actual task masters. Various techniques are available for reducing the numbers of false positives and of false negatives, one of which is increasing the number of items in a test. Such an approach is often appropriate since increasing test items also serves generally to increase the reliability of a test. Interested readers are referred to a recent article by Panell and Laabs (1979), for a further discussion of false negatives and false positives in criterion-referenced measurement.

RECORDING TEST RESULTS

Recording the results of tests is an administrative matter which, if misperformed, can be very costly. Inadequate scoring, inadequate recording, and inadequate reporting may themselves result in misclassifications of the types described above. Test administrators should ensure that all relevant test materials are retrieved after testing. Scoring sheets should be spot checked for legibility. Similarly, additional product or process information that appears appropriate, and that later might be used either for diagnostic purposes or for test improvement, should be recorded at the time of test administration. So should administrator and examinee observations, which may later shed light on improvement of testing procedures or which may affect the reliability or validity of a test. Administrative conditions that result in less than optimal test performance should also be noted and reported (and the procedures subsequently corrected to account for these occurrences). Situations where pass-fail criteria have been inappropriately applied should also be noted and considered for possible revision.

SUMMARY

This chapter has addressed techniques for administering and for scoring criterion-referenced tests. The issue of consistency in test administration is raised, and such issues impacting test control as environmental, personal, and tester variables are discussed. Examples of adequate test instructions for various types of items are provided, as are typical test administration steps and various test situation components which require standardization.

The topic of criterion-referenced test scoring is considered, including such issues as:

- scoring objectivity

- assist *vs*. noninterference types of scoring

- pass-fail scoring

- fixed point scoring

- multiple scoring techniques

Rating techniques are discussed, and an example of a technique for establishing interrater agreement is provided.

Discussion is also devoted in this chapter to the difficult topic of establishing pass-fail cutoff scores for each objective under examination. Classification errors (termed false positives and false negatives), which occur when scoring techniques fail to distinguish masters from non-masters of the subject matter content, are indicated, and a technique for reducing their incidence is mentioned. Lastly, the topic of recording test results is treated.

7

Establishing the Reliability and Validity of Criterion-Referenced Tests

After development and try-out of a criterion-referenced test, it remains for the test to be assessed for two significant psychometric characteristics—reliability and validity—before it can be put to practical use.

THE IMPORTANCE OF
RELIABILITY AND VALIDITY

Test *reliability* refers to the extent to which a test yields consistent scores over repeated administrations. If the same examinees take a highly reliable test more than once, they should score similarly on each administration of the test—assuming no intervening learning, practice, or other method of performance enhancement has occurred between test administrations. Similarly, if individuals score poorly on a reliable test, they should also score poorly on a repeated administration of the test. This type of reliability is known as *test-retest* reliability. Other methods of determining liability also exist, such as "internal consistency" and "split-half" methods; however, such types of reliability measurements are considered less appropriate for criterion-referenced measurement than is the test-retest technique. These other methods are based upon norm-referenced concepts and therefore do not apply as directly to criterion-referenced measurement, as does test-retest reliability.

On a test having low test-retest reliability, examinees who pass on one administration may pass or fail on a second administration merely as a function of chance fluctuations. If a test is not reliable, a a consistency of measurement problem similar to that which might occur if one were to use a faulty thermometer in measuring temperature arises. In one situation, when actual temperature is 20 degrees Fahrenheit, the thermometer may read 15 degrees Fahrenheit. In another, when the actual temperature is 20 degrees, the thermometer may read 35 degrees, and so on. The point is that the instrument is unreliable and therefore incapable of determining correct temperature. Similarly, if an altimeter reads +200 ft. on some occasions when a pilot is 200 ft. above sea level, and +100 ft. on other occasions when a pilot is 200 ft. above sea level, the pilot could certainly not trust the instrument. A malfunctioning altimeter could have disastrous consequences for a pilot, and the same could be true of an unreliable criterion-referenced test.

The second concept discussed in this chapter, *validity*, refers to the extent to which a test actually measures what it purports to measure. For example, consider a multiple-choice, paper and pencil test on electronic troubleshooting procedures that is developed as a low fidelity measure of ability to maintain a sophisticated electronic system. The test may be reliable, that is, it may give similar scores over repeated administrations to the same examinee; however, its validity would need to be determined. In order to establish the validity of such a test, one would have to determine whether people who achieve high scores on a paper and pencil test can in fact accurately perform the specified maintenance tasks. In other words, merely because a test is reliable, does not necessarily mean that it is valid.

The other side of the issue however, is that a test that is not reliable cannot be valid. If a test gives wide score variance over repeated measurements, it cannot consistently measure anything. Consider the malfunctioning altimeter and thermometer in the discussion above. Could these instruments be said to validly measure altitude and temperature? In fact they do not measure anything accurately.

Criterion-referenced tests must be as reliable and as valid as possible. The methodology for construction and administration of criterion-referenced performance tests outlined in this book will aid greatly in ensuring that the tests developed are in fact both reliable and valid. The techniques presented will facilitate "building in" reliability, both by standardizing test conditions and by increasing the numbers of items on a test. The item pool tryout and review processes also tend to increase reliability and validity by enabling selection of the best and most consistent items. Matching test items to the objectives which they are designed to measure on a one-to-one basis also assures test validity.

Yet one cannot necessarily assume that a test is reliable and valid merely because it was constructed carefully. There are many bases of potential error that may creep into test development which may render even the most carefully prepared test unreliable or invalid. The issues of test reliability and validity are critical to accurate criterion-referenced measurement. They are discussed here in order that the reader may more thoroughly understand the concepts and therefore be better prepared to assess the reliability and validity of criterion-referenced tests developed following the procedures outlined in this book.

RELIABILITY

As has been pointed out by a number of authors, particularly by Glaser and Nitko (1971), the appropriate techniques for empirical estimation of criterion-referenced reliability are still at issue. Most techniques for assessing criterion-referenced reliability are exploratory, and are either not fully developed or are based on questionable assumptions. See, for example, Livingston (1972), Oakland (1972), Haladyna (1974), and Woodson (1974). Stanley (1971) has described techniques for applying traditional reliability concepts as developed in norm-referenced situations to criterion-referenced measurement. Popham and Husek (1969), however, have suggested that traditional estimates of reliability are inappropriate in criterion-referenced contexts because they are generally concerned with internal consistency and stability, and that these are inappropriate concepts in criterion-referenced measurement.

A series of works by Livingston (1972 a, b) has suggested that the classical theory of true and error scores can be used to determine reliability in criterion-referenced situations. In Livingston's appraoch to criterion-referenced reliability, each concept based upon deviations from a mean score is replaced by corresponding a concept involving deviations from a criterion score. Livingston, thus, develops a metric by which criterion-referenced reliability can be interpreted a a ratio of the mean square deviations from the criterion score.

Others, principally Harris (1972), have objected to Livingston's application of classical psychometric theory to criterion-referenced reliability measurement. Meredith and Sabers (1972) have also objected to this concept. Lovett (1977), however, in a fashion similar to that of Livingston, has defined criterion-referenced variance as the measure of score variability from a criterion of minimal acceptable performance, and has established a method for computing reliability in terms of an analysis of variance model.

Another reliability model has been presented by Edmonston, Randall, and Oakland (1972), using a metric originally defined by Goodman and Kruskal (1954). Such techniques are for the most part not fully developed (see Oakland (1972) and Woodson (1974 a, b). Additional work is proceeding in the area of criterion-referenced reliability. The interested reader can find discussions of these issues presented by Swezey (1978), and in Berk's book (1980). The practical approach suggested in this book involves the assessment test-retest reliability, a procedure that does not depend upon the internal consistency of test items, and that increases the variability of test results because two test administrations are required. The recommended procedure involves use of a ϕ coefficient for analyzing fourfold data for each examinee (first administration, second administration vs. pass, fail on the test). In the approach recommended here, the ϕ coefficient is considered appropriate (*see* Footnote 1, page 104).

Assessing Reliability

In criterion-referenced measurement, it is necessary that a test be reliable. If a test is found to be unreliable, it is useless to establish its validity, since unreliability, by itself, renders a test inappropriate for use. The issue of criterion-referenced reliability essentially involves the issue of measurement consistency. In assessing the reliability of a criterion-referenced test, using the techniques specified in this chapter, the issue of interest involves the *consistency* of measurement of scores on a test, over repeated administrations. A criterion-referenced test, like any measurement device, involves possibility for errors in judgment. Even with an extremely reliable measuring device, some measurement error will occur as a function of situational constraints and of other operational considerations. Consider, for example, measuring the length of a 2x4 board using a tape measure to measure to the nearest 1/16th inch. Even using a metal tape measure, which is a very highly reliable measuring device, measurement error may occur over repeated trials. If, when measured on one trial, the board measures 10 feet, 8 and 1/16th inches; and on a second trial, 10 feet 8 and 2/16th inches, we know that the actual length of the 2x4 didn't change, and we also know that the tape measure scale didn't change. Such differences in measurement are a function of measurement error. The tape may have slipped a bit on the first trial, or on the second trial, or on both, for example. The extent to which any measurement device, including a criterion-referenced test is consistent over repeated measures, is an estimate of that device's reliability.

Use of ϕ to Estimate Test-Retest Reliability

In developing criterion-referenced performance tests, the issue of test reliability may be expressed succinctly. A test is reliable if examinees who pass it on one administration, pass it on a repeated administration. A test is unreliable to the extent that this is not the case. The same argument can be made for an individual item. To the extent that an item is passed consistently by the same individual(s) on repeated administrations, it is a reliable item. To the extent that this does not occur, the item's reliability is in question.

In Chapter 5, we described how to compute the ϕ statistic for use in item analysis. In that situation, the fourfold ϕ matrix was constructed by establishing which masters passed an item, which masters failed the same item, which non-masters passed the item, and which non-masters failed the item. In this chapter ϕ is also used to compute a simple estimate of test-retest reliability. In order to do this, a group of at least 30 people are required, to whom the test can be administered twice. These people should be sampled randomly from the population of people to whom the test results are intended to generalize (i.e. the people who would ordinarily take such a test as the one under development). In order to establish test-retest reliability, it is necessary to administer the test to the same examinees twice, relatively close together in time. Only about one day should elapse between the first and second administrations of a criterion-referenced test where the purpose is to establish test-retest reliability estimates.

A second important point in assessing test-retest reliability is that the subjects in the reliability sample cannot be informed that they will be retested. The retest must come as a surprise, otherwise the subjects may prepare for the retest during or after the test's initial administration. For purposes of reliability assessment, it is inappropriate for examinees to practice or to study the tasks or skills between the first and second test administrations. Nor is it appropriate for examinees to attempt to recall the test in detail. Test-retest reliability assessment presumes no practice between test administrations, and equivalent testing conditions on both administrations. The equivalent condition requirement applies not only to the specific testing conditions, but also to extraneous and environmental conditions. That is, the retest should be administered at about the same time of day as was the original test; examinees should be approximately equally hungry; at an equal stage of rest; etc., as occurred on the first administration.

To employ ϕ in assessing test-retest reliability, a 2x2 matrix should be constructed in the fashion shown in Table 7-1.

TABLE 7-1

ϕ Matrix for Computing Test-Retest Reliability

		First Test Administration		
		Fail	Pass	
Second Test Administration	Pass	B	A	A+B
	Fail	D	C	C+D
		B+D	A+C	Σ

Note that the ϕ matrix is set up differently than it was for use in item analysis. In assessing test-retest reliability, the matrix is constructed so that the numbers of examinees who passed and who failed are identified for both the first and for the second test administrations. The matrix is filled out by entering in Cell A the number of people who passed the test on both administrations; in Cell B the number of people who failed the test on the first administration, but who passed it on the second administration; in Cell C the number of people who passed the test on the first administration, but failed it on the second; and in Cell D the number of people who failed the test on both administrations. The marginal totals (A + B, C + D, A + D, and A + C) are then computed as was the case with the item analysis matrix. Marginal total A + B shows the number of people who passed on the second test administration, while C + D shows the number who failed on the second administration. B + D shows the number of examinees who failed the test on the first administration, and A + C shows the number who passed on the first test administration. Table 7-2 shows test-retest matrices filled out for two separate tests. These matrices can be used to calculate estimates of test-retest reliability for both tests.

The formula for computing ϕ is the same as was shown earlier in Eq. (5-1):

$$\phi = \frac{(AD)-(BC)}{\sqrt{(A + B)(C + D)(A + C)(B + D)}}$$

(5-1)

Formula for Computing ϕ

Eqs. (7-1) and (7-2) show the ϕ computations for Tests A and B respectively.

$$\phi = \frac{(15)(9)-(5)(1)}{\sqrt{(20)(10)\ (16)(14)}}$$

(7-1)

ϕ Computation for Test A

$$= \frac{130}{\sqrt{44{,}800}}$$

$$= \frac{130}{211.66}$$

$$= .61$$

$$\phi = \frac{(16)\ (8)-(12)\ (4)}{\sqrt{(28)(12)(20)(20)}}$$

(7-2)

ϕ Computation for Test B

$$= \frac{80}{\sqrt{134{,}400}}$$

$$= \frac{80}{366.6}$$

$$= .22$$

As can be seen from Eqs. (7-1) and (7-2), Test A in our example has a considerably higher test-retest reliability coefficient than does Test B. A major issue, however, is the cut-off level of reliability which is considered sufficient in criterion-referenced measurement. No specific answer exists to this question; however, two points of general guidance are suggested:

- A ϕ coefficient of less than +.50 indicates that a criterion-referenced test is of questionable reliability.

- A ϕ coefficient of +.50 or greater, indicates that a test has adequate reliability for use.

Recall that the values of the ϕ coefficient can range from –1.00

TABLE 7-2

Example ϕ Matrices for Two Tests

ϕ Matrix for Test A

		First Administration		
		Fail	Pass	
	Pass	B	A	A+B
		5	15	20
Second Administration	Fail	D	C	C+D
		9	1	10
		B+D	A+C	Σ
		14	16	30

ϕ Matrix for Test B

		First Administration		
		Fail	Pass	
	Pass	B	A	A+B
		12	16	28
Second Administration	Fail	D	C	C+D
		8	4	12
		B+D	A+C	Σ
		20	20	40

through 0 to +1.00. Thus Test A in the example qualifies as a reliable test; Test B does not. The +.50 standard is not rigid, but is general guidance for assessing acceptability of criterion-referenced test reliability coefficients. If, for example, ϕ coefficients of +.48 and +.52 were achieved in a hypothetical reliability assessment case, it would be inappropriate to suggest that the first test was unreliable, and the second one, reliable.

VALIDITY

The final topic in criterion-referenced test development involves the validity of a test. A test that does not measure the appropriate objectives is useless, regardless of its degree of reliability. A test that is reliable, but is not valid, is no more acceptable than is an unreliable test. Three concepts of validity are considered here for the case of criterion-referenced measurement. These are:

- Content validity
- Concurrent validity
- Predictive validity

Each concept of validity addresses in a different manner, the basic validity question (i.e. Does the test measure what it was designed to measure?).

Content Validity

It is generally agreed that content validity is of paramount concern in criterion-referenced measurement. See, for example, Schoenfeldt, Schoenfeldt, Acker, and Perlson (1976); Popham and Husek (1969). A criterion-referenced test may be presumed content valid if all test items are carefully derived from the required performances, conditions, and standards specified in the objectives and if the sample of test items appropriately represents the objectives. (It is also necessary, of course, for the objectives themselves to be sound.) Carefully following the test construction procedures described in this book will enable the development of content valid criterion-referenced tests. The process of determining performance criteria on the basis of information obtained directly from job required skills establishes content validity, that is, performance tests that are derived from appropriate task analyses often provide the best available measure of behavioral objectives. No better criterion typically exists upon which to validate such tests.

Cronbach (1971) has treated the case of criterion-referenced content validity in his discussion of performance testing. According to Cronbach, content validity is a matter of the extent to which a test corresponds to population performance objectives. Content validation is an especially appropriate method in criterion-referenced applications. A test is content valid if the test items are carefully based on the performances, conditions, and standards specified in the objectives, and if the test items appropriately sample the domain of objectives (of course, the objectives themselves must also be sound). Thus in most instances, careful test construction will itself enable the development of content valid tests. However, in certain instances where low fidelity tests are constructed, it may be difficult to determine content validity since items are not likely to be precisely matched to objectives in such situations. [For a variety of considerably different views on content validity, see papers by Schoenfeldt, Schoenfeldt, Acker and Perlson (1976); Tenopyr (1977); Guion (1977); and Klein and Kosecoff (1973)].

Content validity is considered to be the most appropriate validation concept for establishing the validity of criterion-referenced tests. In determining content validity, a test developer systematically checks to determine that each test item measures exactly what the performances, conditions, and standards of the associated objective requires. If all items measure precisely the required performances, conditions, and standards, the test is content valid. If they do not, content validity is not demonstrated. This assumes that objectives have been derived from appropriate task analyses and are themselves, valid. A simple example to clarify this point is shown in Table 7-3.

TABLE 7-3

Example Content-Valid Test Item

Objective	Item
Demonstrate ability to compute a two-way analysis of variance on sample data.	Given the data provided, compute a two-way analysis of variance, correct to the second decimal place using a hand-held calculator. You have one hour to complete this task.

The sample item shown in Table 7-3 provides an accurate example of a content valid item. Actually performing a statistical technique known as a two-way analysis of variance (the test) is obviously the best possible measure of an objective that requires demonstration of ability to compute a two-way analysis of variance on sample data. The example item is therefore content valid by definition. There is no better way to measure the objective than by the test item. If an objective has been established on the basis of actual task requirements, such an item is the best possible way to measure the objective under evaluation. If, for some practical reason, a lower measurement fidelity item is used, the content validity of the test is reduced. Content validity is a matter of the extent to which a test item corresponds precisely to the performance objective upon which it was based. Content validity itself, like criterion-referenced measurement in general, may be viewed as absolute measurement. From an absolute perspective, a content valid test will demonstrate whether an examinee performs an objective to the required standards or not. If test items and objectives are precisely matched in terms of performances, conditions, and standards a test is content valid. If items are not precisely matched to the objectives being examined, content validity is reduced.

In order for a test item to be content valid, the item must represent all aspects of its associated objective. If an objective involves a situation which has three separate aspects, the test item must also address the same three aspects. Content validity is a matter of systematically checking items against objectives. Two basic steps are involved:

- First it must be determined that objectives have been properly derived from adequate task analyses that prescribe clearly what an examinee must do or must know in order to perform the task under examination.

- Second, each item must be carefully evaluated against its associated objective to ensure that the performances, conditions, and standards specified in the item are the same as those required by the objective.

If both checks are affirmative, a test is content valid.

In situations where large numbers of items on a test are associated with a single objective, it is important to establish that each item measures exactly what the objective requires. If objectives have been properly developed and a test consists of high fidelity items based upon these objectives, the test is probably content valid. However, if a test consists of medium or of low fidelity items, its content validity is probably lowered. Thus if a high fidelity test exists, and a systematic check reveals that a test is for some reason not content valid, a major test development problem exists. Some error has occurred during the construction of the test. Either objectives are not properly derived from the appropriate task analyses, or the items do not properly measure the task aspects required by the objectives.

If a test is composed of low or of medium fidelity items, and consequently is not of demonstrated content validity, statistical tests of validity are appropriate. In such situations, the methods of concurrent and predictive validity (which are statistical estimates of validity) may be employed. For example, consider an objective which requires that an examinee be able to attach a removable oxygen cannister to a support bulkhead in a low gravity environment. If the test that addresses this objective requires for practical reasons that the task be performed under normal gravity conditions (which may be the best simulation available), the test is obviously a low fidelity representation of the objective and consequently is not content valid. In such a case, it would be necessary to turn to other statistical concepts of validity estimation such as concurrent and predictive validity.

Concurrent Validity

In determining concurrent validity, test results are statistically compared with an outside measure of the behaviors being tested. The outside measure should be the best available outside assessment of performance on the objective(s) in question. The procedure for establishing concurrent validity involves a statistical comparison (using ϕ) of the test with the outside measure, taken close together in time (concurrently).

Since concurrent validity examines the extent to which an examinee's results on a test compare favorably with his results on some other measure of the performance under examination, it is extremely important that the other measure be the best available external measure of task performance. This is necessary because the external measure is being used as the standard, against which the test is being concurrently validated. A statistical determination of the degree of association between the test and the external measure of performance will provide an estimate of the concurrent validity possessed by the criterion-referenced test. External measures that might be considered for use in concurrently validating a criterion-referenced test include:

- Existing tests already in use

- Existing test data previously obtained

- Supervisor ratings of examinee performance

- Higher fidelity versions of the criterion-referenced test being validated

A criterion-referenced test on first aid performance might be concurrently validated against supervisor ratings of first aid competence or against an existing first aid test which is known to be valid. A multiple-choice test in a given topic area or domain may be validated against a simulated performance test, or against a hands-on performance test in the same domain. It is important to stress that the other measure must be a suitable one. If no appropriate outside measure exists against which to compare a criterion-referenced test, it will not be possible to conduct a concurrent validity assessment of that test.

Once an outside measure (for use as the criterion against which to compare a test) has been established, the computation procedures for computing concurrent validity are relatively simple. ϕ is again the recommended technique. For example, the concurrent validity of a criterion-referenced test on supervisory skills of plant foremen is at issue. Managerial estimates of supervisory skills have previously been used to rate foremen. To establish the concurrent validity of the test, a sample of managers should rate the foremen in terms of their supervisory ability, and the test may then be administered to the same group of plant foremen. Results should be recorded in a 2x2 ϕ matrix such as in the example shown in Table 7-4.

TABLE 7-4

Example ϕ Matrix for Concurrent Validation

		Test Results		
		Fail	Pass	
Result of Manager's Ratings	Acceptable	B 8	A 36	A+B 44
	Unacceptable	D 15	C 1	C+D 16
		B+D 23	A+C 37	Σ 60

The number of plant foremen whose ratings were acceptable, but who failed the criterion-referenced test of supervisory ability is recorded in Cell B. The number of foremen whose managerial ratings were acceptable and who also passed the criterion-referenced test is recorded in Cell A. The number of foremen whose ratings were unacceptable and who also failed the test is recorded in Cell D, and the number of individuals whose ratings were unacceptable but who passed the test, in Cell C. Row and column sums (A + B, C + D, B + D, and A + C) are then computed and Eq. (5-1) for computing ϕ is applied to the resulting fourfold matrix.

$$\phi = \frac{(AD)-(BC)}{\sqrt{(A+B)(C+D)(A+C)(B+D)}} \qquad (5\text{-}1)$$

Formula for Computing ϕ

The ϕ for concurrent validity of the supervisory test thus is:

$$\phi = \frac{(36)(15) - (8)(1)}{\sqrt{(44)(16)(37)(23)}}$$

(7-3)

Sample Computation of
Concurrent Validity

$$= \frac{532}{\sqrt{599,104}}$$

$$= \frac{532}{774}$$

$$= .68$$

The same rule of thumb as was employed for estimating test retest reliability also applies to concurrent validity:

- If the ϕ coefficient for concurrent validity is +.50 or above, the criterion-referenced test is of suitable validity. If the ϕ coefficient is in the range between –1.00 and +.50, the test is of questionable validity.

Two conditions must occur in establishing the concurrent validity of a criterion-referenced test:

- The sample of examinees must be representative of the population of individuals to whom the results of the test are to be generalized. (Random sampling from the population will accomplish this.)

- The sample must be relatively large. (A random sample of 50 to 100 persons is recommended.)

Predictive Validity

Performance prediction using criterion-referenced measures is neither less practical nor more difficult than is prediction using standard norm-referenced measurement techniques. Predictive validity is a particularly appropriate concept in the case of criterion-referenced measurement. Predictive validity involves the same primary assumption as does concurrent validity; the outside measure must be an accurate measure of the performance in question or the validation will be meaningless. Predictive validity is also calculated in the same way as is concurrent validity, except that the outside measure is taken at a later point in time (i.e when the individuals are actually performing the activity for which they have previously been tested). A great deal of work has been accomplished in the area of criterion-referenced test validation. Edmonston, Randall and Oakland (1972), for example, have developed an approach to criterion-referenced test validation that includes both concurrent and predictive validity estimates as is the case with the approach recommended in this book. Such thoughts were initially suggested by Cronbach and Meehl (1955), and by Nunnally (1967). Messick (1975) has also recently presented an argument for this position.

Predictive validity is the extent to which performance on a test is capable of predicting subsequent actual task performance of the examined individuals. Predictive validity is based on the same concept as is concurrent validity, and can also be estimated using the ϕ coefficient, in the same way. Unlike concurrent validity, however, predictive validity compares an examinee's result on the criterion-referenced test with his performance on an external performance measure taken at a later point in time. Whereas the test administration and the outside measure of performance are obtained close together in time for estimates of concurrent validity, periods of six months or greater may intervene between the time the test is administered and the time that the second sample of job performance is obtained for use in estimating predictive validity. Predictive validity estimates therefore are often used to determine the extent to which results on a criterion-referenced test actually predict results on the job or task that the test was developed to assess. Typical types of external measures used in predictive validity estimation (i.e. to be predicted by the criterion-referenced test) include:

- External ratings of on-job performance
- Other existing job proficiency tests
- Objective indices of job proficiency such as: number of products produced, quality of work performed, and number of mistakes committed

The predictive validity of a test may be estimated by employing precisely the same ϕ technique as was used to estimate concurrent validity. It may, for example, be decided to validate a criterion-referenced test of leadership skills against outside ratings of the individuals' leadership performances taken at a later point in time. The same general rule as for reliability and for concurrent validity also holds for predictive validity:

- A ϕ coefficient of +.50 or greater indicates an appropriate level of predictive validity for a criterion-referenced test.

The same cautions that apply for concurrent validity also hold for predictive validity:

- The validation sample must be relatively large

- The validation sample must be representative of the population to which the test is intended to generalize

- The outside measures (the criteria) against which a test is validated must be the best appropriate measures available, not merely the only measures available

To the extent that any test is validated against an inadequate criterion, the validity of the test will be lowered. If an adequate outside criterion against which to validate a criterion-referenced test does not exist, an index of predictive validity cannot be computed.

DEALING WITH TESTS HAVING LOW RELIABILITY AND/OR LOW VALIDITY

If the empirical indices of validity and/or reliability (i.e ϕ coefficients) are inappropriately low, a criterion-referenced test may not be suitable for use as an actual measure of performance proficiency. A test is considered to have acceptable reliability if the test-retest ϕ coefficient is +.50 or greater. Content validity in criterion-referenced measurement is demonstrated if the performances, conditions, and standards in each test item match, on a one-to-one basis, the performances, conditions and standards required by the objectives that the item(s) are designed to measure.

To the extent that data such as those required by these guidelines do not occur, a criterion-referenced test will probably be inappropriate for its intended use. If a test, or items within a test, are modified in order to create a higher reliability and/or validity index, the reliability and/or validity of each modified item (as well as of the entire test containing the modified items) must be reassessed using the techniques described in this book.

Suggestions for modifying a criterion-referenced test to increase its validity and/or reliability include:

- It is often possible to increase the reliability of a total test by adding items. Again each item must match the performances, conditions, and standards of the objectives that the item is intended to measure. If a test is designed to measure several objectives simultaneously, appropriate proportions of items to objectives must be maintained in the test. Review the test plan development techniques described in Chapter 3 to determine this proportion. If items are added, test-retest reliability as well as concurrent and/or predictive validities must be recomputed.

- A test that is not content valid as a function of low fidelity items cannot be made content valid merely by reconstructing the items in a higher fidelity format. It may be necessary to modify practical constraints in order to achieve this objective, or it may be necessary to modify the convenience of administration; however, a valid test which is less convenient to administer is dramatically preferable to an invalid test in any situation.

- If it is determined that test reliability or validity is low because of use of an inappropriate subject sample in computing the reliability and/or validity indices, reliability and/or validity may be recomputed upon readministration of the test to a different, more appropriate sample. The sample must, of course, be appropriately large and representative of the population to which test results are intended to generalize.

Criterion-referenced tests must also be administered in a properly standardized fashion. It is however, possible to keep readministering tests until one or more of the numerous administrations demonstrates an acceptable level of reliability and/or validity. Such a process is obviously totally inappropriate. Readministration of a criterion-referenced test and recomputation of reliability and/or validity indices are appropriate only if serious errors were made during the first administration. A criterion-referenced test must be completely reassessed for reliability and validity if modifications are made to the items, to instructions, or to performances, conditions, or standards.

SUMMARY

In Chapter 7, issues involving the establishment of reliability and validity of a criterion-referenced test are discussed. In the case of reliability measurement, a specific type of reliability (known as test-retest reliability) is advocated in criterion-referenced measurement. According to this concept, examinees who score well (or who score poorly) on one administration of a criterion-referenced test should score similarly upon retesting. To the extent that such results occur consistently, test-retest reliability may be said to occur. A relatively simple, practical approach for assessing test-retest reliability, which employs a phi (ϕ) coefficient for analyzing fourfold data for each examinee (first administration, second administration $vs.$ pass, fail on the test) is suggested. Numerous examples of calculating ϕ coefficients are provided. In the approach recommended in this chapter, it is suggested that criterion-referenced reliability ϕ values of lower than +.50 indicate questionable test-retest reliability.

In the case of validity assessment, three concepts for use in establishing the validity of a criterion-referenced test are considered. These include: content and concurrent and predictive validity. It is generally agreed that content validity is the most appropriate validation concept for establishing the validity of criterion-referenced tests. Content validity is defined as the extent to which all text items address precisely the performances, conditions, and standards specified in each objective, and to which the sample of test items appropriately represent the objectives. Several examples of content validity in criterion-referenced testing are presented.

If a test is composed of low or of medium fidelity items, and consequently is not of demonstrated content validity, two statistical validation techniques are recommended. In such cases the methods of concurrent and of predictive test validation are recommended. In both these forms of criterion-referenced test validation, the test results (i.e. pass, fail) are compared with an outside measure of performance effectiveness, taken either close together in time (concurrently) or at a later point in time (predictively). Again, a simple phi (ϕ) coefficient approach is recommended (i.e. pass, fail on the test $vs.$ acceptable, unacceptable outside evaluation results). Tests having ϕ coefficient results of below +.50 are considered to be of questionable concurrent or predictive validity.

Finally, a discussion of how to deal with tests having low reliability and/or validity is presented. Several suggestions for modifying a criterion-referenced test to increase its validity and/or reliability are described.

References

1. Adams, J. A. On the evaluation of training devices. *Human Factors*, 1979, 21, 711-720.

2. Berk, R. A. (ed.). *Criterion-Referenced Measurement: The State of the Art.* Baltimore, Md.: Johns Hopkins University Press, 1980.

3. Boyd, J. L. and Shimberg, B. *Handbook of Performance Testing: A Practical Guide for Test Makers.* Princeton, N.J.: Educational Testing Service, 1971.

4. Chenzoff, A. P. and Folley, J. D. *Guidelines for Training Situation Analysis (TSA).* Port Washington, N.Y.: Naval Training Device Center, 1965. NAVTRADEVCEN 1218-4.

5. Cronbach, L. J. Test validation, in Thorndike, R. L. (ed.) *Educational Measurement.* Washington, D.C.: American Council on Education, 1971.

6. Cronbach, L. J. and Meehl, P. E. Construct validity in psychological tests. *Psychological Bulletin*, 1955, 92, 281-302.

7. Denova, C. C. *Test Construction for Training Evaluation.* New York: Van Nostrand Reinhold/American Society for Training and Development, 1979.

8. Edgerton, H. A. Personal communication, 1974.

9. Edmonston, L. P.; Randall, R. S.; and Oakland, T. D. A model for estimating the reliability and validity of criterion-referenced measures. Paper presented at the annual meeting of the American Educational Research Association, Chicago, 1972.

10. Fine, S. A. and Wiley, W. W. *An Introduction to Functional Job Analysis.* Kalamazoo, Mich.: W. E. Upjohn Institute for Employment Research, 1971.

11. Fishbein, M. and Ajzen, I. *Belief, Attitude, Intention, and Behavior: An Introduction to Theory and Research.* Reading, Mass.: Addison-Wesley, 1975.

12. Frederiksen, N. Proficiency tests for training evaluation, in R. Glaser (ed.) *Training Research and Education.* Pittsburgh: University of Pittsburgh Press, 1962.

13. Glaser, R. Instructional technology and the measurement of learning outcomes: Some questions. *American Psychologist,* 1963, 18, 519–521.

14. Glaser, R. and Nitko, A. J. Measurement in learning and instruction, in R. L. Thorndike (ed.) *Educational Measurement.* Washington, D.C.: American Council on Education, 1971, 625–670.

15. Goodman, L. A. and Kruskal, W. H. Measures of association for cross classification. *American Statistical Association Journal,* 1954, 49, 732–764.

16. Graham, D. L. An examination of the feasibility of using criterion-referenced measurement in large scale survey testing situations. Paper presented at the annual meeting of the American Educational Research Association, Chicago, 1974.

17. Guilford, J. P. *Fundamental Statistics in Psychology and Education.* New York: McGraw-Hill, 1965.

18. _____. *Psychometric Methods.* New York: McGraw-Hill, 1954.

19. Guion, R. M. Content validity—The source of my discontent. *Applied Psychological Measurement,* 1977, 1, 1–10.

20. _____. Principles of work sample testing: III. Construction and evaluation of work sample tests. Alexandria, Va.; US Army Research Institute for the Behavioral and Social Sciences Technical Report 79-A10, 1979.

21. Haladyna, T. M. Effects of different samples on item and test characteristics of criterion-referenced tests. *Journal of Educational Measurement*, 1974, 11:2, 93-99.

22. Hambleton, R. K. Testing and decision-making procedures for selected individualized instructional programs. *Review of Educational Research*, 1974, 44, 371-400.

23. Harris, C. W. An interpretation of Livingston's reliability coefficient for criterion-referenced tests. *Journal of Educational Measurement*, 1972, 9, 27-29.

24. Hively, W. W.; Patterson, H. C.; and Page, S. A universe-defined system of arithmetic achievement tests. *Journal of Educational Measurement*, 1968, 5, 225-290.

25. Klein, S. P. and Kosecoff, J. Issues and procedures in the development of criterion-referenced tests. Princeton, New Jersey: Educational Testing Service, ERIC TM Report 26, September, 1973.

26. Livingston, S. A. A classical test-theory approach to criterion-referenced tests. Paper presented at the annual meeting of the American Educational Research Association, Chicago, 1972(a).

27. _____. A reply to Harris' an interpretation of Livingston's reliability coefficient for criterion-referenced tests. *Journal of Educational Measurement*, 1972, 9, 3(b).

28. _____. Criterion-referenced applications of classical test theory. *Journal of Educational Measurement*, 1972, 9(1), 13-26 (c).

29. Lovett, H. T. Criterion-referenced reliability estimated by ANOVA. *Educational and Psychological Measurement*, 1977, 37, 21-29.

30. Lyons, J. D. *Frameworks for Measurement and Quality Control*. Alexandria, Va.: HumRRO Professional paper 16-72, 1972.

31. Mager, R. *Measuring Instructional Intent, or Got a Match*. Belmont, Calif.: Lear Siegler/Fearon Publishers, 1973.

32. _____. *Preparing Instructional Objectives*. Belmont, Calif.: Lear Siegler/Fearon Publishers, 1962.

33. Mager, R. and Pipe, P. *Analyzing Performance Problems, or 'You Really Oughta Wanna'.* Belmont, Calif.: Lear Siegler/Fearon Publishers, 1970.

34. McNemar, Q. *Psychological Statistics.* New York: John Wiley & Sons, Inc., 1962.

35. Meredith, K. E. and Sabers, D. L. Using item data for evaluating criterion-referenced measures with an empirical investigation of index consistency. Paper presented at the annual meeting of the Rocky Mountain Psychological Association, Albuquerque, 1972.

36. Meskauskas, J. A. Evaluation models for criterion-referenced testing: Views regarding mastery and standard-setting. *Review of Educational Research*, 1976, 46, 133-158.

37. Messick, S. The standard problem: Meaning and values in measurement and evaluation. *American Psychologist*, 1975, 30, 955-966.

38. Miller, G. A. The magical number seven, plus or minus two: Some limits on our capacity for processing information. *Psychological Review*, 1956, 63, 81-97.

39. Miller, R. B. Task description and analysis, in R. M. Gagné (ed.) *Psychological Principles in System Development.* New York: Holt, Rinehart and Winston, 1966.

40. Nunnally, J. C. *Psychometric Theory.* New York: McGraw-Hill, 1967.

41. Oakland, T. An evaluation of available models for estimating the reliability and validity of criterion-referenced measures. Paper presented at the annual meeting of the American Educational Research Association, Chicago, 1972.

42. Osborn, W. C. An approach to the development of synthetic performance tests for use in training evaluation. Alexandria, Va.: HumRRO Professional paper 30-70, 1970.

43. _____. Process versus product measures in performance testing. Paper presented at the annual conference of Military Testing Association, San Antonio, October, 1973 (b).

44. Osburn, H. G. Item sampling for achievement testing. *Educational and Psychological Measurement*, 1968, 28, 85-104.

45. Panell, R. C. and Laabs, G. J. Construction of a criterion-referenced, diagnostic test for an individualized instruction pro-

gram. *Journal of Applied Psychology*, 1979, 3, 255–261.

46. Pearlstein, R. B. and Swezey, R. W. Criterion-referenced measurement in the Army: Development of a research-based, practical test construction manual. Alexandria, Va.: U.S Army Research Institute for the Behavioral and Social Sciences Technical Report TR-78-A31, 1978.

47. Popham, W. J. (ed.). *Criterion-Referenced Measurement: An Introduction*. Englewood Cliffs, N.J.: Educational Technology Publications, 1971.

48. Popham, W. J. and Husek, T. R. Implication of criterion-referenced measures. *Journal of Educational Measurement*, 1969, 6, 1–9.

49. Sanders, R. J. and Murray, S. L. Alternatives for achievement testing. *Educational Technology*, 1976, 17–23.

50. Schoenfeldt, L. F.; Schoenfeldt, B. B.; Acker, S. R.; and Perlson, M. R. Content validity revisited: the development of a content-oriented test of industrial reading. *Journal of Applied Psychology*, 1976, 61, 581–588.

51. Sherman, M. and Zieky, M. (eds.) *Handbook for Conducting Task Analyses and Developing Criterion-Referenced Tests of Language Skills*. Princeton, N.J.: Educational Testing Service, 1974.

52. Shoemaker, D. M. Toward a framework for achievement testing. *Review of Educational Research*, 1975, 45, 127–147.

53. Swezey, R. W. Aspects of criterion-referenced measurement in performance evaluation. *Human Factors*, 1978, 20(2), 169–178.

54. _____. Toward the development of realistic measures of performance effectiveness. *Journal of Educational Technology Systems*, 1977, 5(4), 355–367.

55. Swezey, R. W. and Pearlstein, R. B. Developing criterion-referenced tests. *JSAS Catalog of Selected Documents in Psychology*, Spring, 1975, 5, 227.

56. Swezey, R. W.; Pearlstein, R. B.; and Ton, W. H. Criterion-referenced testing: A discussion of theory and practice in the Army. Arlington, Va.: U.S. Army Research Institute Research Memorandum 75-11, December 1975.

57. Tenopyr, M. L. Content-construct confusion. *Personnel Psychology*, 1977, 30, 47–54.

58. U.S. Army Training Support Center, Individual Training and Evaluation Directorate, *Guidelines for Development of Skill Qualification Tests*. Fort Eustis, Va.: 1977.

59. Woodson, M. I. C. E. The issue of item and test variance for criterion-referenced tests. *Journal of Educational Measurement*. 1974, 11, 63–64. (a).

60. _____. The issue of item and test variance for criterion-referenced tests: a reply. *Journal of Educational Measurement*. 1974, 11, 139–140. (b).

Index

A

Accurate condition specifications, 27-29
Acker, S. R., 149, 150, 165
Adams, J. A., 161
Administering and scoring criterion-referenced tests:
consistency in test administration, 123-127
recording test results, 136
scoring techniques, 127-136
Ajzen, I., 4, 162
Aspects of objectives, 32-40
clarity of intent, 34-36
performance indicator simplicity, 36-38
precision, 39
unitary objectives, 32-34, 38
Assist scoring, 128-129

B

Behaviorally anchored numerical scales, 68, 70, 78, 132
Berk, R. A., 8, 103, 144, 161
Boyd, J. L., 9, 15, 161

C

Checklist, 67, 68, 78, 131, 132
Chenzoff, A. P., 24, 161
Clarity of intent (objectives), 34-36, 41
Clearly stated performance objectives, 26-27
Completion items, 59-60, 77
Components of an adequate objective, 25-30

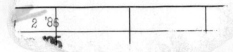